ENDORSEMENTS

D1495203

"After 35 years of Army service I thought I knew a little bit about soldiers and their families. My work with Lou and Linda proved over and over again...I only knew a little bit! I cannot commend highly enough the contents and masterful insights into our forces and family struggles and triumphs. Lou gives us more than a treatise on soul damage, he shows us his soul as well. I know of no one else with this heart grasp, humility, and wisdom. We are all the better for it."

Colonel Mike Hoyt, Chaplain U.S. Army (Ret.)

"I am a blessed man in every way. I am loved by God and my family, and respected by the people I work with in my company. I am also Humpty Dumpty; I have PTSD and have received superb treatment (physically, emotionally and spiritually) that allows me to be highly functional and happy. I believe this book will be a help to those people (psychiatrists, chaplains, counselors, pastors, lay people and family members) who labor to enable a warrior to heal successfully."

Colonel David Hale, U.S. Army (Ret.)

"As the wife of an Army Veteran with PTSD, *Tending the Warrior Soul* has an insight that can only be achieved through a deep desire to help the warrior. I can never walk in my warrior's shoes, but only come alongside when he lets me. Warriors need to be able to wrestle with Christ and understand what His blood meant in a far different way. *Tending the Warrior Soul* helps me remember my job is to 'listen, pray and search the scriptures.'"

Mrs. Carole Hale

"George Washington once said that, 'a nation will be judged by the way it treats its veterans.' If this is true, then those of us who are concerned with the care of souls have no greater responsibility than to stand with them on their journey with their God. Lou Harrison is a skilled and dedicated servant of God. His wisdom will be an asset to any who desire to understand."

Chaplain (Major) Brian Koyn, 75th Ranger Regiment

"I have known Lou for many years now and I gladly call him my friend. He knows the value of earning someone's trust. I have struggled with some things that happened during an Afghanistan deployment. This book is the single best manuscript I have read on the subject of post-combat-related issues. I highly recommend it to anyone dealing with war issues."

"Josh," a currently active Marine Corps Special Operations SGT

"Lou and Linda Harrison have faithfully and fruitfully ministered to military people and their families through

Cadence International for nearly fifty years. This reason alone should compel you to eagerly and carefully read *Tending the Warrior Soul*. Out of these years of relationship with military people, Lou has composed a thoughtful and tender exposition of the warrior's soul. This is not just a book of good and helpful ideas; it is primarily an expression of deep wisdom and incarnational love. Lou's words emerge from a caring heart for our wounded warriors. This book is congruent with the man I know – wise, humble, loving, and thoughtful. And, if you read reflectively you will also find help for your own heart. Most of us have never experienced the trauma of war, yet we all know some level of soul wounding in this broken battlefield of life. I know it is Lou's prayer that this book not only increase your confidence in how God can use you to love our wounded warriors, but also that it would stir your hope for healing in your own soul and all those dearest to you. To these ends, I highly recommend this labor of love from Lou Harrison to you."

David Schroeder, President, Cadence International

TENDING THE WARRIOR SOUL

L OUIS H ARRISON

Cover Design by Craig Jentink
Cadence International

Copyright © 2013 by Louis Harrison

Tending the Warrior Soul
by Louis Harrison

Printed in the United States of America

ISBN 9781628392517

All rights reserved solely by the author. The author guarantees all contents are original and do not infringe upon the legal rights of any other person or work. No part of this book may be reproduced in any form without the permission of the author. The views expressed in this book are not necessarily those of the publisher.

Unless otherwise indicated, Bible quotations are taken from the NEW AMERICAN STANDARD BIBLE ®, COPYRIGHT © 1960, 1962, 1968, 1971, 1972, 1973, 1975, 1977, 1995 by The Lockman Foundation. Used by permission. www.Lockman.org.

www.xulonpress.com

DEDICATION

For the glory of God
Through the saving grace of our Lord Jesus Christ
By the guidance of His Holy Spirit
That His love and grace may be poured out
upon the souls of our faithful warriors

FOREWORD

Ministry to war experienced troops begins and ends with a servant's heart. This is not about "fixing" people. Servants live alongside their charge, accepting the hardships and traumas of the other as the conditions of being useful. Ministry to warriors begins, not with them but with the minister, with us. We must "remake" our worldview, expand our theological reference points, and accommodate our civilized views about violence, cruelty, right and wrong to the uncivilized applications of war. Neither God nor His commandments change, for these are the anchor points, trustworthy and sure. What does change are the size, depth, and ferocity of the ocean we once envisioned.

War is, in fact, hell. The minister who serves under those conditions accepts another level of preparation of his own heart and psyche that is foreign to civilian experience. Ministry to warriors is necessarily transformative to the minister to be a servant. Reading on war, understanding its vocabulary, and appreciating the terrible split-second decisions of combatants and the massive strategic decisions of commanders are vital.

Looking at the management of violence and balancing the nobility of soul in the circumstances of destruction is unnatural. Listening to the anguish of a guilt-ridden battle survivor or hearing the despair of a haunted sniper is unparalleled. Teaching people to sort through the reality of God while sifting through the ashes of soul, spirit, and mind burned in the consequences of war is not "routine" business.

This book is about ministry, servanthood, and the ultimate transforming power of God. It does not propose biblical templates to answer all questions or explain war actions or identify God's specific will in a fallen world. It is about two primary things: God's character, and man's.

We believe God is sufficient in character, principle, and personal relationship to redeem mankind's worst failure, war, and its impact. We do not propose what that looks like in every situation, only that any situation willingly surrendered in faith to God's sovereignty will prevail to God's glory and our eternal benefit. Faith is not evasive, nor is it ill-informed. Faith is the evidence of things hoped for and the conviction of things not seen...and without faith, it is impossible to please God.

Colonel Mike Hoyt, Chaplain, U.S. Army, Retired.

INTRODUCTION

In war there are *traumas to the soul* that are not assuaged for the warrior by even the most excellent psychological care, medical interventions, and official support programs.

The purpose of this book is twofold:

- **To advance our understanding of this "soul damage."**

- **To offer support, encouragement, lessons from personal experience, counsel, challenge, and resources to those God has placed alongside our warriors for the care of their souls, as well as to the warriors themselves and their loved ones.**

I acknowledge that this is a relatively narrow focus of ministry, considering the immense breadth of spiritual need and ministry opportunity across our armed forces.

I understand this because my wife and I have had the privilege of serving all branches of the military over the past forty-seven years, and many of those years have been invested in their lives through open-home hospitality ministry including singles and families, combatants and non-combatants, teens and children. We have loved this ministry, and still love and value it.

However, for the past thirteen years God has increasingly placed us alongside, and drawn our hearts specifically to, *combatants*...the ones who now carry the label, *"warriors."* I believe this ministry focus is God-ordained, that is to say I did not "envision" or "pursue" it out of any advance awareness of what I have now come to see is a truly special need. We have simply obeyed God and followed Him into what may now be fairly called a "passion."

The reality of combatants routinely standing on the doorstep of death and deliberately knocking on the door for the sake of us non-combatants has simply taken hold of my heart. Years ago, my brother, a career police officer, told me of an event in his life I'll never forget, that gives a visual and very personal face to this. At a point early in his career he was dispatched to a house where it was supposed there was a wanted fugitive. He knocked on the door, and as it was flung open from the inside, he found himself looking directly into the barrel of a pistol. Honestly, I don't recall how he handled this particular situation, which was *one event* out of a twenty-nine-year career. I only know that when he told me the story, it stunned me and left an indelible mark on my spirit. This uniformed guardian who confronted death on behalf of his community by knocking on that door, was *my brother*!

Something like that feeling has happened to my spirit regarding the young people we send "to knock on the door" of death as the guardians of our national and personal safety. These are our children; our brothers; our family!

My focus on the **soul damage** *they come away with on our behalf is not to neglect or ignore the physical and emotional-psychological harm they experience. In fact, the opposite is true.* Dedicated and disciplined care for the traumatic and stress-induced harm they experience is crucial ministry in itself; **and it is a pathway to understanding the spiritual damage their soul is experiencing.**

I admire and honor the vast resources of physical and emotional care that are being invested in them by official, contractual, and volunteer caregivers. This kind of care is being provided for our warriors even as far forward as their combat outposts.

*However, as I've listened, studied, and labored with combatants, I've found that **biblically based, fearlessly applied soul care** for them is not as vast. And where it is available it is not often taken advantage of by the warriors.*

I believe this relative void in ministry to the soul damage in warriors exists for a variety of reasons, including official constraints on specifically Christ-centered biblical ministry in some contexts, and a lack of connection, understanding and engagement by many caregivers in and around military communities. This is an obstacle I desire to help God's servants overcome, on behalf of our warriors.

1.

"SOUL DAMAGE?"

The *soul damage* our warriors experience is the main burden of the book, but it's not a generally used term; nor is it a concept addressed in military mental health vocabulary. I recently read an article referring to "moral injury," which described a particular aspect of damage to the soul —specifically the *guilt* that is caused by *moral failure* in war. This is a genuine and important concern, but it is only one dimension of the harm done to the soul by war.

I'm also aware of an author who speaks of Post-Traumatic *Soul* Disorder. However, he refers to the soul from a psychological, rather than biblical, perspective.

Becoming aware of the harm done to the human soul by the conduct and impact of war is *essential* and *foundational* to everything that follows here, and to all helping ministry to warriors, **because it is rooted in what God has revealed about Himself, our human nature, and our relationship to Him.**

15

Followers of Christ and ministers of His faithful and true Word need to discern *both aspects* of the trauma and post-traumatic harm done to combatants by the horrors of war:

1. The *physical* and *psychological-emotional* harm, and
2. The *spiritual* harm that is *always present*...sometimes apparent and sometimes hidden in the soul.

Although officially supported care for traumatized and stressed warriors *does* make reference to the "spiritual dimension" of the warrior, *he is guided to consider his spirituality as an open set of religious and spiritual options.* Chaplain Mike Hoyt shares his perspective of this, drawn from his personal involvement in the Army's efforts to address the "spiritual fitness" of the warrior:

"In 2009, the Army pursued an initiative called Comprehensive Soldier Fitness. The focus was on a more holistic approach to resilience as the force faced the tremendous strain of long and repeated deployments. One of the five dimensions attempted to address spiritual fitness. It was a noble effort but remained unattached to any form of theology or doctrine. The warrior was sent forward with the vague advice to 'hunt the good stuff, to find what feels good personally as a spiritual individual, and then protect and nurture that feeling.' It is merely humanism with

16

a 'spiritual' face. The good news in this approach is that the spiritual dimension is officially recognized as an essential part of wellness and resilience. The other news is that the vague advice is about as good as it can get in order to keep the secular institution of the US government and Department of Defense from violating the establishment clause of the First amendment."

Thus, the *official goal* of this perspective is the warrior's psychological restoration and strengthened resilience. Both are noble goals, and both leave matters of the *soul* unaddressed. I am deeply pained by the emotional-psychological suffering our warriors experience. Being conversant with the issues through academic training in psychology and counseling, I certainly understand and deeply desire the warrior's psychological restoration and strengthened resilience. However, I know from both education and personal experience that the war-harmed soldier may be helped back to his feet physically and emotionally, and restored to the fight, or to his home community, *while a hidden spiritual battle still rages irreconcilably within him.* We must not be like the prophets and priests of Jeremiah 8:11, who *"heal the brokenness of... my people superficially, saying, 'Peace, peace,' but there is no peace."* A Special Operations Chaplain friend adds this decisive thought about giving superficial spiritual assurances: *"It will shut down any warrior if we tell him he is all right and he knows he is not all right."* As Jeremiah mourned for Israel

(8:21-22), we mourn for the brokenness of our warriors, but then we set our hearts resolutely to guide them to the One who is the "balm in Gilead," that their relationship to God — their *soul health* — may be established.

God declares that we were originally created in His image.

> *"God said let us make man in Our image, according to Our likeness...Then the Lord God formed man of dust from the ground, and breathed into his nostrils the breath of life; and man became a living being."*
> *Genesis 1:26, 2:7*

Although our relationship with Him is corrupted by sin and His image in us is marred, yet our *awareness of God continues,* through the activity of conscience, the evidences seen in His marvelous creation, and exposure to His revealed Word (Romans 1:19-20). *Because of this awareness, the conduct of war — the taking and forfeiting of human life — inevitably creates spiritual conflict within the warrior.*

Chaplain Hoyt shares his thoughts regarding this:

> *"The experience of war attacks all of one's senses and heightens one's awareness of God even, and more often, especially, when the very idea of a loving God seems inconceivable. Participants in war were sinners before the war, and most knew it well. War, however, confuses what was known about sin and in one of war's cruelest ironies makes one's soul all the more*

aware of God. This is at the heart of soul-damage. One's view of the image of God is what is at stake. God as He is. Warriors as they are. The ministering person must be able to perceive the image of God even more carefully to include: God, warriors, and themselves. And then do the extraordinary, enter into those images as selflessly as possible... and serve for Christ's sake and the soul of the warrior. What I am talking about is dealing with that 'continuing awareness' of Romans chapter 1. The scripture calls it 'that which is known about God... His invisible attributes... clearly seen through what has been made, so that they are without excuse.' That is the impossible conflict of being human before God; we are all without excuse. What can one do or say when WAR in its unlimited languages of experience bids us carry an entirely new repertoire of 'excuses'? **The conduct of war inevitably creates spiritual conflict within the warrior that requires much more than 'hunting the good stuff.'"**

Just a cursory scan of the thousands of references to soul and spirit in the Word of God reveals that it is not that we *have a soul*, but that *we are living souls, with abiding awareness of God, Who is our Creator and Judge.*

When psychologists refer to our self-consciousness they use the term, "psyche." The term recognizably comes from the Greek, "ψυχή," which is usually translated in the Bible as "soul," or "life." But the passage I'll quote in a moment is exemplary in that Jesus' own use of it grants understanding that the soul is not merely the seat of our psychological self-awareness, but our very existence as an accountable being before God. In the passage, Jesus deliberately switches His use of the term *"soul"* from meaning our *sense* of individual psychological meaning and value in life, to refer to our *life and accountable existence before God.*

This matters greatly to our understanding of the harm done within the warrior that **underlies** the more evident physical and emotional-psychological damage.

In the three synoptic Gospels, *Jesus reveals two crucial things for our understanding:*

1. The *danger* the soul *senses* and *actually faces* in judgment, *if the soul's desires are chosen over self-denial and following Christ*; and
2. The reality that the *soul* or *psyche is* our very life and *accountability to God.*

It is in Luke's rendering of the passage, chapter 9:23-26 that Jesus lays out the sobering truth:

"If anyone wishes to come after me, he must deny himself, and take up his cross daily and follow me. For whoever wishes to save his life (ψυχή) will lose it, but whoever loses his life (ψυχή) for my sake, he is the one

*who will save it. For what is a man profited if he gains the whole world and loses or forfeits **himself**."(The word in the original here is **"himself,"** not, "his life.")*

The point is that there is a *spiritual awareness in the warrior* that there is *danger in war...not merely to his physical and psychological state*, but to the state of his eternal *being, which was created, and will be judged by God.*

If he finds it difficult to talk about the psychological pain he's feeling, **how much more difficult to speak of the spiritual danger he fears**, which he may not even have words to express.

Thank God for the many who pour themselves into physical and psychological restoration of the warrior. And yet *he may be alone in his spiritual conflict—in the solitary confinement of his soul, bereft of visitation, help, and hope.*

This conflict *is **compressed into the unarticulated question: "Where does my soul, my life, my very being, stand before God right now? And how does this affect my eternal destiny?"***

The conduct of war attacks this inward awareness of God and ultimate judgment from a bewildering number of angles within the warrior. The issues that arise may be different for the believer than for the unbeliever, or they may be similar in some cases — but they do arise just as surely for both.

Further along, I'll give examples of this from the lives of warriors themselves, those who have learned to function adequately physically, emotionally, and relationally in the military, in their families, and in their communities; but who *still confess that they are afraid to face God or to talk to Him.* In the case of one of my friends, *his way of resolving the conflict in his soul has been to choose to stop believing in God.* Meanwhile, those who care for him continue to pour labor, skill, and intelligence into trying to set him free from the emotional conflict that is actually *rooted beneath the level of these efforts... the soul conflict* that can only be resolved between himself and God.

How does our compassionate Savior view the warrior's soul damage, in comparison to the physical and psychological damage he's suffering?

In the familiar story of the healing of the paralytic man, in the synoptic gospels – Matthew 9, Mark 2, and Luke 5, *Jesus Himself reveals His perspective of soul healing in relationship to physical/psychological healing.* He does this by His handling of the paralyzed man.

As we read the passage our usual focus is naturally on our admiration of the faith and determination of the man's friends, and on the confrontation of Jesus by the accusing scribes.

But there is a moment when we thoughtlessly leave the feelings of the paralyzed man himself entirely out of the discussion. In fact, *Jesus Himself sets aside the man's physical anguish for the moment*, while He makes His point about His Divine authority to His religious antagonists.

Think of it! The man was paralyzed, helpless, longing with all his heart for the healing of his crippled body; and his friends promise him, *"One way or another, we'll get you to Jesus*, and He will heal you!"* Imagine the hope that welled up in his heart as his faithful friends slipped past the crowd, tore out a section of the roof, and gently lowered him into the immediate presence of the great Healer.

Now lie on the pallet with this poor broken man as he hears Jesus compliment his faith and that of his friends, and then hears Him lovingly say, *"Son, your sins are forgiven."* Then Jesus calmly turns to confront the scribes and Pharisees and argue against their evil denunciations.

"What??! Wait!! What about my *broken body?*!"

What was the paralyzed man thinking and feeling at that moment? "Does Jesus care only about my sins? Does He care nothing for my broken body? Why did I come here? Am I supposed to be excited that my sins are forgiven as my friends carry my useless body home on my pallet?"

Thankfully, we get to hear the rest of the story as Jesus turns back to him and commands him to pick up his pallet and walk. *But we must recognize* that in that emotionally terrifying moment, *Jesus did in fact declare His priority*: the *relationship of a man with God is of the first and utmost importance.* For a fearful moment, Jesus left his body broken. *But He did not for a moment leave his soul hopeless.*

In another context Jesus said it with brutal plainness. With reference to *anything* that might hinder a man in his relationship with God, He says in Mark 9:43, "…it is better for you to enter life crippled, than, having your two hands, to go into hell…"

This is not a lesson we callously preach to a physically or emotionally wounded warrior. But it is a lesson we must understand, or we risk "healing him superficially."

This, then, is what I think of as the essence of *soul damage*…this spiritual guilt, distress, doubt, fear, anxiety, confusion, conflict, anger, and frustration, all of which are connected to the warrior's sense of his *relationship to God, His righteousness, and His judgment.*

Chaplain Hoyt reminds us of the overwhelming influence of combat on the warrior King David who, under orders from God, underwent transformation from a gentle, psalm-composing shepherd boy, to a cowering embodiment of war's transforming influence (Psalm 32:1-5) who, by his own testimony, had to be crushed by God to be restored:

"Even though God clearly commissioned David to fight battles and lead wars for His purpose David was eventually rejected from building the temple he spent a lifetime amassing wealth and resources to construct. Why? Is God so unfair? No. There are no holes in God's soul. The hole was in David's. The violence he lived through tore at his being until eventually he developed a hole so big in his soul he conspired and committed premeditated murder, adultery, and perjury.

War changes people, even good people. The concern for the ministry is not over the cause of the warrior's involvement, obedience is honorable. The concern is the personal cost to the soul and who is mending the tears, and how.

"It is this concern that provides the only basis for ministry and intervention. The one who enters into the injured soul of a person whose dreams, expectations, and faith system are now war-torn does so only with great fear and trembling, not judgment. Fear that the minister would remain worthy of the intimate trust of restoration. Trembling in soul and spirit at the anguish of another and the responsibility that love in Christ places upon those who accept His mantle of leadership. 'For though I am free from all men, I have made myself a slave to all that I might win the more… to the weak I became weak that I might win the weak; I have become all things to all men, that I may by all things save some. And I do all things for the sake of the gospel, that I may become a fellow partaker of it.'" (1 Corinthians 9:19-23)

Even the most extreme damage to the soul *can be healed*; and we can help if we understand the warrior himself, and serve him in the spirit of the Apostle Paul.

2.

WHO *IS* THE WARRIOR?

Those of us desiring to minister to war-damaged troops from a biblical perspective ought to be disciplined in preparing ourselves to help in their recovery by reading, listening, and every other available means of *learning to **know** them*.

I use the word "warrior" as is usually done today to represent the military member who has been involved in combat. But this is with a sad awareness that there are many who are not designated combatants, and yet have been deeply traumatized by involvement in war. Among these are the medical support staff — some of whom are actually engaged in combat, and some who daily labor in the relentlessly gory environment of trauma centers and intensive care units — and even the spiritual helpers themselves, military chaplains, who often plunge unarmed into the pit of battle with their soldiers. They may have held the bloody hands of wounded and dying warriors while they poured out their hearts to God for them, or led too many heartbreaking memorial services for "their boys."

A heartbreaking example of this for me was a "green-side" (assigned to the Marines vs. a "blue-side," assigned to the fleet) Navy chaplain I met at Camp Pendleton. He was overwhelmed with excitement to meet his Marines' spiritual needs in combat in Iraq.

Not long after his battalion was deployed, I saw a photo of him in a Marine Corps Journal article. I was not surprised to see him *running* to join a unit of his Marines as they headed out on a mounted patrol. After months of combat the regiment, with his battalion, returned to Pendleton. In conversation with the Division Chaplain I learned that this great young chaplain was suffering from such severe emotional trauma that it had left him unable to continue in ministry. I didn't have further contact with him, but my heart ached to think of the pain that was wrenching a *soul* so abandoned to the spiritual care of his Marines. Though he went into the battle unarmed, he was certainly a spiritual *warrior*.

Since there are many others who are well prepared to help warriors with their temporal and psychological needs, those of us involved in ministering the Word of God to members of the armed forces and their families ought to be *constantly* and *explicitly* searching for *biblical* understanding of "who they are," the issues they face, and God's means of healing their traumatized *souls*.

God has allowed us the privilege of serving these men and women in a time of war. Let's be as well prepared as we can be.

I've found that part of my preparation is to gain insight into how the war-fighter *views himself or herself*. There's a reason I've used the term, "war-fighter," at this point. As I write further, I'll continue to mainly use the word "warrior" for brevity, and also because it has become the acceptable term of honor used by the command, the media, and the public for the one engaged in warfare on behalf our country.

However, I've observed that *not everyone who fights on our behalf would necessarily wish to be described or defined as a warrior.* It's possible that one who has fought in war — even one who has been injured in the fight — may find it inappropriate or undesirable to identify with this term. A thoughtless assumption on our part may hinder us at the outset in our attempt to help. Genuinely honoring the war-fighter requires that, even in this respect, we *know* the person we seek to serve.

America has been served by an all-volunteer military since 1973, the close of the Vietnam War era. Therefore, it's probably reasonable to assume that almost all who wear the uniforms of the various service branches today do so with conscious commitment to the defense of our country, even at great cost to themselves.

It's also probably appropriate to assume that *almost* all of those who are required to engage in the actual physical fighting of war are doing so by their conscious and willing choice. *However, this is **not always** so.*

Listen to these abbreviated quotes from a warrior-medic friend:

*"You'd be surprised how many corpsmen in FMSS
(Field Medical Services School) felt tricked into
joining the Marines...I can't help but think of Doc S....
He likely had no more than 2 weeks of exposure to his
platoon before we left for theater. He rode in the back
of the vehicle without windows and never got out...
(he) was often criticized for the way he wore his gear,
not oriented around his weapon, but his med bag. A
few times he came to me disgusted with the behavior
of his Marines...last I checked (he) was...living in the
wilderness of Colorado."*

So, in seeking to minister to their damaged post-combat
souls, it's clear that there is a potentially significant difference
between the *attitudes* of some of those who *willingly and
faithfully* serve in combat, those who may *hesitantly* serve,
and others who *eagerly hunger for the fight*...whether this
eagerness is "bred" into them by training, or comes with them
from home and streets. This difference of attitude can make
a great difference in both the *nature of the impact* war has
on their emotions and souls, and on *their particular way of
responding to our attempts to help.*

I think, for example, of some young men I've known who
came from urban streets where gang violence was common.
These that I'm referring to joined the infantry, where their vio-
lence-influenced background was built upon and intensified as
they were taught to think of themselves as "trained killers,"

and taught to *crave* the fight. All infantrymen are taught to "run to the sound of the guns." This is codified in the mission statement that they are to *"close with and destroy the enemy and/or his ability to fight."*

As a result, some have personalized this and amplified it to the level that they can't wait to get out there and "get some."Of course, this attitude is often adjusted in them by the painful realities of warfare. But still the effect of war on this young man's emotions and his soul may be very different from the effect on one who came from a rural environment, attended church regularly in his community, and enlisted in a combat MOS (Military Occupational Specialty) out of a sense of duty and love for country, or to honor a family tradition.

In his book, *Outlaw Platoon,* author Sean Parnell describes two of his squad leaders in a way that puts personal faces on the varied backgrounds of the "warriors" and the potentially different effects of war on their emotions and souls. With wise perceptiveness he identifies first the man he believes to be a "born warrior whose spirit and character are forged for the fight," and then the other, who fights because there is no other solution. He fights with purpose and idealism, but without pleasure, and when the task is completed he gladly returns to family and home life.

In our efforts to minister the truth and grace of God to their war-damaged souls, we may find one of these men in a state of hardened anger with a tendency to violent reactions and little conscious remorse; while we may find the other in a state of remorse, guilt, confusion, and anxiety. Or, as a warrior friend says, this latter person may experience both conditions, possibly because of the confusion. Some, he says, *"can be almost bi-polar with their disposition."*

The obvious summary of these comments is, again, if we desire to minister meaningfully to these warriors we must learn to *know* them *as they are.*

Historically, we have generally used the term, "warrior," with reference to those whose "occupation," or "profession" it is to fight. In our recent popular use of the term *we may have thought of it purely in its defensive or protective meaning;* but I think the term has generally signified a more aggressive and proactive connotation. Its common historical use has referred to inter-tribal or international *conquest.*

So in our counseling with the man who has chosen the *occupation* of combat, to refer to him as a warrior may suggest honor and validation, and it may possibly open a door of communication for us in our attempts to help him in his struggles... because certainly warriors, even in this connotation of the word, do experience soul damage.

On the other hand, to thoughtlessly use this term in conversation with a young man who serves voluntarily and with honor but without any desire or intent to continue in combat as a profession, it may mislead our understanding of the *particular* pain he's experiencing. And it *may not be particularly inspiring for him to reveal to us what's really going on in his heart.*

We have in our uniformed armed forces, and under contract to our government, those who for perfectly honorable reasons have chosen to be our protectors — our dedicated **professional** *warriors*. Among them are those in our various Special Operations commands. I believe we should honor them and give praise to God for them. I've learned, however, that we must also recognize that their backgrounds, their approach to the *idea* of war-fighting, their training, and their *attitudes* toward war's *effects on them* are usually very different from those of our "non-professional" war-fighters, however dedicated, well trained, and effective they may be. When they write or speak of themselves they use terms like, "a particular breed," "confident," "warriors in every sense of the word," and "intensely private when it comes to team business." They think of the word, "warrior" as virtually sacred and some may rankle at society's casual use of the term with reference to athletes, businessmen, or politicians. I read one author's assertion that, because of this confident, aggressive approach to combat, it is *rare* for the most elite special operators to be *diagnosed* with PTSD.

One brief example of this was the response of a Special Forces soldier to an SF chaplain friend of mine who tried to speak to him of his need for the Lord. His reply was, "I didn't need God to get through Selection, why would I need Him now?" He apparently did not yet understand that his need for God was not primarily in the realm of his physical, mental, and emotional *performance*, but in the eternal realm of his *soul...* his *accountability* to God.

The true warrior is to he honored for his powerful service to the country. And yet, the brutality of war *does* touch and affect even this warrior's soul. The book I'm reading as I write these words is the personal story of a highly decorated Navy SEAL Corpsman who persevered academically to become a physician's assistant and then returned to combat. His story includes his own eloquent account of his battle with Post-Traumatic Stress Disorder. However, unsurprisingly, I observe that in the spirit of the elite warrior, and with his medical background, he managed to deflect the *diagnostic use* of the PTSD term with reference to himself. Speaking to such warriors of the damage their *soul* sustains through combat is a radically different thing from speaking to a combatant who does not *define* himself as a warrior.

It seems that almost everything about the life and thoughts of a Special Operations warrior is ratcheted to the limit, and tuned nearly to the breaking point. The good news is that, in keeping with this level of intensity, many of our most elite professional warriors do profoundly acknowledge their trust in God and His presence in their lives.

I recently had the honor of attending the promotion in rank of a Special Forces chaplain friend. Many of the men in his battalion were present. He *knelt before all* and asked that we pray for him in the sense of a re-commissioning for service. A good number of the SF soldiers in his battalion gathered around him, laid their hands on him and prayed for him. I was moved and honored to be among these men in prayer. This was no, "God bless our Chappy," prayer. These men prayed thoughtfully and deeply in the unique and powerful Name of Jesus, Lord and Savior, while their warrior brothers — believers and unbelievers — looked on or joined in silent prayer.

God grant that we may *know* the warrior soul we serve.

I work at trying to grasp these distinctions to be as effective as possible in ministering to these distinctively different men and women. But for brevity and for the honor that is intended by it, I'll resume referring in my writing to all of our war-fighters as warriors.

3.

"LABELING" CONCERNS TO BE AWARE OF ON BEHALF OF THE TRAUMATIZED WARRIOR

Why do I call "labeling" a "concern" in this conversation with Christian *soul-caregivers?* And why is it necessary or useful to say anything more than simply, *"Be cautious and sensitive about using labels in conversations with, or about, warriors"?*

The answer is as I've repeatedly urged: *in every way, and in all dimensions of their experience possible, we need to **know** the warrior we serve.*

Knowing him in this aspect of his post-traumatic experience only **begins** with guarding ourselves against getting tripped up with labels and distracted from our spiritual task. The labeling process *will go on* in a variety of ways, from a variety of sources, and it may affect him (as it has many) in ways he himself doesn't understand and can't control. Helping him navigate this unmarked spiritual minefield may be one of the facets of soul care he needs from us.

Understanding the warrior involves being alert to what he may be experiencing in the therapeutic and emotional recovery process, including the *spiritual bewilderment* sometimes experienced through labeling and treatment. In his book, *Battle Ready, Memoir of a SEAL Warrior Medic,* the SEAL medical officer I referred to above agonizingly described his own emotional and spiritual bewilderment. As he guided other warriors through their PTSD care, he struggled to understand the right way to get help for himself. He battled against overmedicating himself, knowing he needed help for his "problem," but not responding well to his assigned counselor, and all the while fearing that in the process he was losing his faith in a sovereign God.

Among our war-harmed troops, there are those who are so deeply traumatized that combat-induced issues rise to the level of *"disorders."* Medical and mental health officials generally define this condition as extreme, persistent, post-traumatic symptoms, which reveal changes and "imbalance" in brain chemistry. Because the term "disorder" is a psychiatric (that is, medical) diagnosis, non-medical spiritual-caregivers sometimes effectively quarantine themselves from playing their essential role in the warrior's healing because they feel unqualified to minister to one with a "disorder."

Based on the testimonies of the warriors themselves, as well as that of the research physician from whose expertise I draw helpful understanding, it's even possible that a warrior may be experiencing negative physical symptoms from the treatment he's receiving, and struggling with knowing how to address it.

Medical care providers are working in the area of their expertise and are generally not engaged in providing guidance in the spiritual issues that accompany the physical damage they're treating. Ministers, then, *should be* engaged with the warriors in this process.

Some post-traumatic *symptoms* may be similar for all warriors. However, all do *not* experience the same kinds and degrees of trauma. In fact, they experience the *same kinds of trauma* in *different ways* — ways that are unique to their backgrounds, personalities, training, and spiritual understanding.

Medical doctor and researcher, Dr. Harry Croft, co-author of the book, *I Always Sit With My Back To The Wall,* helps us understand this by describing the functions and interactions of the brain's main regions, and pointing out that the **thinking-deciding** part of the brain is not the part of the brain that has immediate control over the body's post-traumatic stress **reactions**. Thus, the part of the brain *that initiates stress responses* is *not initially* under the *conscious control* of the person; so a person under the influence of post-traumatic stress responses may find that the symptoms don't immediately go away simply because he decides to "get over it." Medical treatment may be needed to bring the symptoms under control while they are being addressed at the cognitive (thinking-deciding) level through counseling.

In his book, *Dr. Croft then speaks directly to the warrior,* alerting him that the medical treatment he is receiving is *complex and potentially risky. It is not a "cure," but rather the management of the symptoms* (anger, re-experiencing, depression, anxiety, nightmares, etc.) *through the use of a variety of drugs.* This is intended to be helpful until psychological counseling becomes possible and potentially effective. In this section of his book, Dr. Croft extensively details the complexity and risks of the drugs, and he cautions that there is *not yet a single medication that generally treats all the symptoms of the PTS-Disorder.*

He expresses the concern that he has seen many veterans who seem overmedicated or under-medicated for their condition. Thus, he strongly cautions the PTSD sufferer that the use of medications should always be a collaborative effort between the warrior and his physician, and that he should speak candidly with his physician about how he is doing with his medications.

It's a tall order to urge this degree of understanding and interaction with medical staff, especially for a young, traumatized grunt, whose normal response will be to go silent and try to "suck it up." Your warrior friend may need help with understanding and communication in this confusing situation, as well as dealing with his fear, and finding hope.

Everyone who experiences actual combat is impacted by combat operations with some forms and degrees of trauma. However, the application of labels can potentially contribute to the warriors' struggles. Here are a couple of examples of how this has, in fact, happened. A soldier becomes discouraged because he has a label announcing his "problem," but the medical system is overloaded and he's *not getting* the medical help he's been told is his primary means of stabilization. Or a soldier came home with a latent rage in his soul, and the only help he finds is a *label and an ever-increasing dosage of drugs, leaving him in a stuporous state to conduct his daily work and relationships.*Marine SSGT Jeremiah Workman, recipient of the Silver Star for bravery in combat, describes his struggle with this latter issue in his book, *Shadow Of The Sword.*

Army Lt. Col. (Ret.) Dave Grossman, author of several important books on war, including his foundational work, *On Killing,* is troubled by the negative self-fulfilling prophecies sometimes created by the public's assignment of labels to returned combatants.

Referring to what he calls "The PTSD Trap," he says that sensational journalistic statements can encourage our returning warriors to become trapped in self-pity by exaggerated "news pieces" implying that every veteran is suffering from full-blown PTSD. Referring to an article in an April 2009 *Scientific American*, he shows that *by looking for PTSD,* it's actually possible to *cause it.* Creating negative impressions of our warriors who may have come home with some degree of emotional damage only adds to their sense of self-doubt, making their attempts at even such tasks as finding a good job daunting, thus leading to even more serious issues.

I've also noticed that there are "well-intentioned"(?) private agencies that essentially treat combat trauma labels as a financial windfall. Recently I saw an ad run on television by a trauma recovery agency that tried to sell itself with the exaggerated claim that the VA says fifty percent of our warriors return from deployments with PTSD. I've never seen such a statistic published by the VA or by any military branch; nor is it consistent with what I've seen in personal experience. Rather, it is an example of what Dave Grossman refers to, and of the risks related to unwise labeling.

A Special Operations friend shared some pretty intense comments with me about the inherent dangers in this labeling issue. I'll quote him, but leave him anonymous. You'll understand why.

> *"If we continue to create this victim mentality, then the only ones who will come forward are those who have bought into it. I find myself constantly making judgments about those who get interviewed on TV or magazines. With many, I immediately think, 'He is a dirt bag. He was a dirt bag before the war and now he is one with a diagnosis.' I usually have to repent and realize he is hurting in his own way and was hurting long before he joined the Army. I also make judgments when I hear someone whose 'life was wrecked by PTSD after a yearlong deployment to Kuwait.'*
> (Quotes added by me, to highlight my warrior friend's irony, for readers who may not know the 'dangers' of this

kind of deployment) He continues: *The more these types are thrust into the limelight and get to be the spokesmen, the more problems we'll have in getting the warriors to try to ease their pain."*

The sum of these thoughts on labeling concerns is simply this: *the assignment of descriptive terms and treatment of the traumatized warrior is useful, as it is in any other diagnostic process. But it's also possible for it to contribute to a whole new set of perplexing problems for him as he struggles toward emotional and spiritual healing and restoration. We who are committed to his full healing — body, soul, and spirit — need to be aware of this dimension of the process, and prepared to help him traverse it.*

4.

HELPING THE WARRIOR UNPACK AND SORT OUT HIS SPIRITUAL "BATTLE RUCK"

The warrior's dealing with his *physical* "battle ruck" (pack) on return home provides a helpful analogy for understanding and helping him "unpack" the **emotional** and underlying **spiritual** ruck he carries home with him from combat.

By this I mean taking the steps to begin to open up the pack of memories and experiences, considering them in the presence of God, dealing with them in appropriate ways, and putting them away.

The unpacking and sorting can evoke everything from laughter to unbearable pain or shame.

Some never unpack, but rather throw the bag in a corner and try not to look at it. One Army SGT put it succinctly:

"...it scared me to look in my ruck. I did not want to see what I had done or re-live it."

This is also reflected in words I've heard from others, "You don't understand, I was a bad person in combat!" When a warrior who has been engaged in actual combat says, "I was a bad person," he doesn't mean he had to kill an enemy and he feels bad about it. He means he did things he knows he shouldn't have done even in kill-or-be-killed combat. He means he did things that he knew were wrong by *anyone's* standards...things that, in his heart, he hopes will never come out of the ruck and be exposed to the light. And yet there they hide in the dark corners of his soul, and he has no idea how to unpack them or what to do with them. These are spiritual issues, needing resolution between the warrior and his Creator.

A warrior friend illustrates this in graphic terms:

"It's like being exposed to pornography for the first time, part of you it bothers and part of you it exhila-rates. Many of my Marines would say combat is better than sex. Dance with the devil and the devil never changes, he changes you."

For any warrior, the process of *beginning* to unpack can, in itself, bring on guilt and doubt... "What right have I to be unpacking at all, when my brothers are still out there in the fight?" Pages could be filled with quotes to this effect from the men. I don't think this is exactly the same as "survivor guilt," because his brothers may not have been killed...yet. It's as if just unpacking is an act of betrayal, a kind of abandonment of his brothers.

Some start unpacking and then the unpacking slows down because it becomes harder to face some of the stuff they find. My Navy Corpsman friend who served in hard combat with a Marine Light Armored Recon unit gave me his desert hat, and I think the fact that I valued it actually helped him in a small way as he began the emotional-unpacking process. But for him the task goes on, and even today — more than six years later — there's stuff he's still working on unpacking that's hard to pull out and deal with. Let me share a recent example of this from this same friend, arising after years since combat. This part of his unpacking process may have a very positive result as God leads him on.

My friend's mother had recently been diagnosed with terminal cancer with no hope of a cure. She was especially discouraged by recent scans, and was now being forced increasingly to face her imminent death. My friend told me that, as he was sympathizing with her by phone, he commented to her that he understood her feelings because he has gone through something like what she was experiencing. I was a little surprised that he said this, and I asked him to tell me about it.

For the first time, he told me that during brutal, deadly combat in Iraq *he became convinced that he was not going home alive*. I've learned that this is not an unusual inner battle for warriors to face, but it was the first time he had mentioned it to me.

He told me of the fear and the bargaining; (*"If I can get a hand or leg blown off, I can at least go home alive."*) and he talked about the resignation that then morphed into hard, lasting anger. This anger only intensified in combat, and it was this anger that he brought home with him and vented on others. Today he says, ***"It's a frustrating and confusing place to be in your head when you've accepted your own death and then you're back in the U.S. You're back to "normal" life.*** *When (in Iraq) I'd tell myself, 'I'm already dead, I'm just getting the living ones back home,' I felt like I had purpose."*

When he finished talking about it, I shared with him what had become clear to me, and my understanding of why he dared to tell his dying mom he had felt what she's feeling. What he was doing in Iraq was going through the grieving process. He was grieving his own death in advance of its occurrence…just as his mom was now doing.

His response to what I said was quietness, as he reflected and absorbed. I encouraged him to go forward in this conversation with his mom… after first asking the Lord to help him embrace the reality that God had — after all — spared his physical life, even though it seemed some part of him had died in Iraq. In the unique understanding of the warrior he could minister to his mom, who *would* die unless God intervened miraculously.

Since the previous paragraph was written, his mom has passed into the presence of the Lord. He was with her when she died, and later shared a moving tribute to her at the memorial, including a clear witness to the *saving Life of Christ*.

Clearly then, some combat "gear" (like the hat) can be cleaned up and put away without too much trauma. But there may be some that is bloody — with someone else's blood or the warrior's own — that's heart-rendingly painful, or morally frightening, to touch.

For example, speaking of his combat in Iraq, my friend says:

"I took a red and white checkered scarf with bloodstains still on it (he didn't mention the source of the scarf or the blood), put it in a small gear bag called a butt pouch that attaches to a load-bearing vest. It's in a storage unit in Alaska. Occasionally I think, 'I should do something with that.' But I can't decide whether to honor it, burn it, or simply throw it in the trash. For the most part I've forgotten about it. I may have looked at it twice since I put it away six years ago."

Some of what's in a warrior's spiritual ruck may never see the light of day. Without wise and godly help it may fester in his heart and lead to deep, long-term grief in his soul that a "stranger" will never know.

Here's how a friend of mine — a recently retired Army Intelligence Colonel — put it in a Veteran's Day message:

> *"There is a point where no matter how righteous or warranted the kill, no matter how evil the foe, there is a point where it is too much. I am not trying to sound unpatriotic; I am very patriotic. I am just trying to explain how some of those soldiers at the extreme edge carry a different burden than others.*
>
> *"One friend told me, 'I signed up to defend my country, not to kill, and kill, and kill.' Another said, 'I don't want to be thanked, I want to be forgiven.' A big problem is, those that feel the most that way, will never say a word. They are too ashamed. They will never acknowledge they have killed anyone much less forty or fifty."*

Proverbs 14:10, 13 tells us *"The heart knows its own bitterness and a stranger does not share its joy... Even in laughter the heart may be in pain, and the end of joy may be grief."*

If we're alert, compassionate, and prepared, we can help the warrior God brings our way to open up, deal with, and put away the stuff from his ruck that he either allows us to see, or that he can't hide. Eventually, he may allow us to help him with the deepest, most untouchable stuff.

At Ft. Drum during Operation Anaconda, we had 10th Mountain Division Infantry soldiers attending our Hospitality House. Those who were close to us mostly went with the flow of the program — Bible studies, home-cooked meals, fun activities, etc. There were also obviously traumatized "drop-ins." I tried — without understanding — to get them to talk about their experience in combat in the mountains of Afghanistan during Operation Anaconda, that early, hard fought attempt to capture or kill Osama Bin Laden. But I only got what I later learned were typical "grunt" responses: "lousy leadership;" "those guys (the enemy) can't shoot anyway, they just 'pray-and-spray;'" "we were well trained tactically, but then they used us in a way that threw it all out and made us sitting ducks in a shooting gallery;" etc.

I've learned that these responses are carefully designed to maintain *emotional* distance, which in turn keeps *soul* issues even more deeply buried and inaccessible.

A warrior friend tells me of another, more brutal, emotionally distancing behavior. He says:

> *"I knew marines that wanted to talk about their kills, describe them. A fellow scout in my platoon would even tell stories about how he shocked family members at get-togethers when one of them was stupid enough to ask him if he had killed anybody."*

I regret now that I failed to get to *know* and *connect* with my 10th Mountain soldiers well enough to minister to their war trauma more deeply and effectively. With a busy schedule of Bible studies and activities, and some combatants *seemingly* calmly involved in our Hospitality House ministry, I just didn't get it. Perhaps others in ministry are experiencing the same thing today that I was at that time. **How could I help a warrior "unpack" if I remained a "stranger," just a bystander, while he deals with his hidden pain?**

I needed to find ways to *pursue* the warriors — both those who seemed to be calmly participating in our routine ministry activities, and those who needed help but were normally beyond our reach.

One of the things I would do differently now in that context, and in any ministry where there are both combatants and non-combatants involved, is to deliberately carve the time out of our busy schedule to include some group activity that is exclusively for combatants. And I would try to find ways to *pursue* combatants as I did later with young Marines on the streets of Oceanside, California.

This would be structured not as "group therapy," nor even as a "Bible study for combatants," but as an exploration together of their experiences, coupled with a search for light from God's Word. It would start with my asking them to *teach me what I'm missing — what God needs to do in my own heart* to make me a trustworthy person, a worthy guardian of the things they need to pull out of their ruck, and a capable spiritual guide in how to handle it and what to do with it.

It's a well-known fact that warriors talk most freely *with one another* after combat, and that's important. But the benefit of this doesn't usually go beyond letting off steam and affirming one another or, even less usefully, resorting to drinking and fighting. A Marine friend told me that his former platoon-mates want to have a reunion (the surviving ones — several have died in combat since he left active duty). He desperately wants to join them in the reunion, but is terribly conflicted. He's trying to stay free of alcohol and he says the only way the reunion can end is in boozing and fighting.

To unpack and effectively deal with the deeply dirty stuff, they need *spiritually wise and understanding guidance.*

In humbly pursuing the effort to help them unpack their spiritual ruck, here are some things we must learn not to be:

- **Glib** – For example, I actually heard an elder lay counselor call after an infantryman who was on his way out the door of the servicemen's center, "Just memorize John 3:16 and you're in!" Actually, that's such an extreme example it may risk distracting from the main point, which is: ***almost any comment or response that springs immediately from our unbloodied minds will seem cheap and clichéd to the warrior.***

- **Presumptuous** – We deceive ourselves if we hear a complaint and think we "understand." I've seen that this is true even for one who has experienced war. The bitterness in every heart is unique, influenced by an as-yet-unknown number of factors. Humbly probing (when welcomed), listening, and responding non-judgmentally from the heart, will eventually bring insight and open the warrior's heart to *relevant and life-changing* guidance from God's Word.

- **Preachy** – Most warriors have heard more sermons while growing up than you realize…more, in some cases, than they cared to hear. The majority of our infantrymen are from Texas and other parts of the southern U.S., where they've been well "churched." They've probably heard all the corrective verses we can think of to quote…and a lot of them have deliberately walked away, although most have their "I'm saved" shields up, to fend off preachers. Aggressively pressing scripture texts on the warrior, then, is demeaning to him, just as it is when someone does it to you or me. Our friendship and kindness are the scriptures in action that will begin to build trust. Genuine open conversation will lead to knowing the warrior and offering suitable spiritual counsel in due time.

- **Intrusive** – Warriors emphasize the offensiveness of this behavior. Who am I to step into their painful thoughts? It shouldn't be too difficult for *any of us* to look inward for a moment and discover some sensitive or painful situation in our personal or family life, where someone who is not an intimate friend would not be welcome to blunder around asking questions or offering advice.

Stay focused on caring, until he decides he can trust you enough to invite you in. It's not hopeless, however; and we take encouragement from these words by a friend who is an Army MAJ, Ranger, combat troop leader. He says: *"By sharing your life you gain the right to be heard. By listening, praying and being guided by the Holy Spirit you can discern the true spiritual issues."* He won't mind if I add that, we first have to earn the right even to *listen* — to *hear* the warrior's account of his pain.

- **Merely curious** – Apart from famously insensitive questions like, "Did you kill anybody?" there are plenty of ways we can shut the door of the warrior's heart in our own faces. *It helps to first look into his countenance, and ask myself the question, "Am I ministering to him, or merely to my own curiosity with the questions I'm thinking of asking?"* Questions about killing and its impact on his soul may one day be suitable and valuable, but *never* from a *merely curious* "stranger."

- **Easily offended** – for a man who has been engaged in actual combat operations, the language and interpersonal activities of the world he's been in are not "civilized." He will scrub his vocabulary around civilians in social settings, but if you begin to probe his war-altered heart, it will evoke what's really there and what's hurting. It's not pretty, so be ready, or else it would be better not to try to step into his hidden hurt.

There's something I've learned about this subject that may seem strange or careless, but believe me, I'm not careless about this subject. Rather, it's because *I care so much* for these men that I have the perspective I'm about to describe.

I'll say it straight out...the infantry, whether Army or Marine Corps, *has adopted a cultural dialect.* The dialect has a relatively small vocabulary, used for any expression of excitement, anger, or enthusiasm, and most is vulgar and offensive. *But it is the language of the culture in which they have come to live and relate,* and they speak this language as the accepted means of communication within the group. Profanity, they sense, is *fundamental to integration and acceptance.*

I'm not speaking foolishly or suggesting that they don't know the difference, or even that they can't control it... because they *do* control it when they need to. But this is, in fact, the dialect of their tribe, their "brotherhood," and when they are with their brothers most of them shift into it without any deliberate intent to be "bad" (to sound "tough," yes, at times) but not usually to deliberately display moral degradation.

I recently had a believing friend, now separated by years from his combat experience, walk me though some videos of his Marine unit's actual combat experience. As he described the situations, he unconsciously reverted to the "dialect." When I probed this with him afterwards he first had a slight look of surprise and puzzlement, and then sincerely told me that he wouldn't have known any other way to describe the scenes than in the language of the moment.

This uniqueness of the warrior's experience and relationships may be the reason for the ironic and interesting fact that, although I've been constantly exposed to this dialect in person, and in the many books I've read by and about the infantry in combat, their language does not infect my speech. I never find myself slipping and using their words. It's *their* dialect, and I don't speak it.

Of course, in my prayers for them I have considered the question, "Then, doesn't it *matter* that they use such language?" Certainly it does, and there are some — both officers and enlisted — who rise above it through: an unusual level of *spiritual commitment, educational habit,* or *even pride.* But I know that few of these young men have, or choose to use, such resources, and we must reach them where they are.

On occasion, a warrior has *approached me* about this issue of language and behavior because of his own personal conviction. Many of those who are followers of Christ struggle with it. One Marine came to me literally *cursing himself* for his bad example as a believer!

Here are the words of a warrior friend:

"I remember when I approached you about this prior to going to Iraq and while I was still rejecting Christ as Lord. I asked you if it bothered you. You said yes. Then I asked why you never corrected me on it. Your reply was pretty key for me and though I can't quote it I'll do my best. You told me that correcting my language wasn't important right now, getting me to love Jesus was, and if I accepted Jesus he might lay it on my heart to clean up my language. I know that this sounds simple but coming to the place in my head that 'I clean up my language because I'm a Christian' not 'I clean up my language to become a Christian.'"

When the warrior approaches me about this, we talk about overcoming in the strength of the Spirit of God, about rising above the culture, being strong in the Lord and swimming against the cultural current, setting the example as followers of Christ, praying and filling their minds with the Word of Truth, and other encouragements and exhortations.

I've also tried to direct their attention to the lives of infantry leaders they respect who have set the example of rising above, and I've encouraged them to emulate that example of humble courage in the face of infantry culture. A warrior friend who recently read this last sentence did something touching and powerful...at the end of my sentence he simply added in parentheses the *name* of such a friend.

And yet, while they are immersed in the culture, especially in combat operations, I've known few who were able to so radically depart from the cultural world of their brothers. Routinely, in their self-expression in books about their combat experience, they casually flow between vulgar language and references to their "Christian faith." (I want to talk about their "faith" and their understanding of "spirituality" further on.)

Vulgar language is not unique to combatants. In fact, it is growing more common in our society. However, in society at large it is not as definitively a cultural "check point," or means of acceptance. To the young warrior it is an element of integration and acceptance. How we attempt to communicate with them in this context may make or break our efforts to reach them and lead their damaged *souls* — not merely their speech — to spiritual newness.

A Special Forces MAJ friend — a strong believer whom I've never heard use vulgar language — says:

"Your practical advice... was very good. I absolutely agree that you have to earn the right to listen... and then do a lot of listening! You were absolutely right about not judging them on non-essential issues (like the example of cussing above). Military men (especially men in active combat) are by nature coarse and earthy men. The environment they have been in and the things that they have had to do and see have made them live in a very unique 'culture' of men. To get offended 'initially' by cussing, disturbing comments, disturbing actions, disturbing life choices... would shut the door to any meaningful relationship with most of these men. From their perspective, the items just mentioned are not 'big issues' to them, so they can't be big issues to the counselor either, or you will never be invited to hear about the "heart" matters.

"A perfect example of this was during this last trip. I had the joy of being able (by the work of the Spirit) to participate in leading one of my men to a saving knowledge of Christ. In the weeks that followed his conversion he kept wrongly assuming that I was judging him on his (foul) language...I didn't realize he was thinking this until one day, when he finally

brought it up. I was able to encourage him and tell him that God and I loved him for who he was, and that his language was not an issue right now. We talked about focusing on understanding God's grace and transforming power in our lives. I have never seen a man so relieved to not be judged for cussing for the first time in his life. He was discovering a New God! One that cared about his heart! And would ultimately transform him to be more like Christ. He understood that his language would get better over time, because of the power of the spirit in him, and no longer because of imposed human "behavior modification" and guilt.

"I think that your awareness and warning…was good. Embarking on a journey with combat veterans is messy, gritty, difficult, and sometimes very disturbing. It is certainly not for the faint of heart. But I am so glad you have put so much thought into this, because these men (and women) so desperately need godly men and women to walk with them through these very difficult journeys of 'unpacking' their baggage…"

In Sebastian Junger's book, *War*, there is a kind of humorous example of the "grittiness" we need to look past to see into the heart of the warrior. He tells of a period of time when the Combat Outpost where he was embedded with an infantry platoon had been involved in a lot of fighting. Stress was increasing among the soldiers, despite an "enormous" amount of psychiatric support.

He describes a moment when a soldier sidled up to him, sat on an ammo crate, and gave him an awkward grin. He knew this was probably leading up to a confession, and sure enough the soldier admitted he'd only been there four months, and couldn't believe how "messed up" he already was. He confessed that he had gone to the counselor for advice and the counselor's question was whether he smoked cigarettes. When he answered, "no," the sage advice he received was, "Perhaps you should think about starting." Then the soldier lit a cigarette and inhaled. "I hate these...things, he said."

Compared to the other things we need to "learn *not* to do," this final comment on *not being easily offended* has been long. It has been mostly focused on loving the warrior in the face of vulgar language. This emphasis is because spiritual caregivers are aware of scriptural warnings against abuses of our speech and our bodies, and these can be (have been) barriers to true ministry to the warrior. But Jesus Himself showed us what our response should be. He knew in advance of Peter's vulgar denial; and then He *heard* with ears of purest holiness, Peter's words in the courtyard of the high priest as he, *"... began to curse and swear, 'I do not know this man you are talking about!'"* Mark 14:71 After His resurrection, when He presented Himself to His disciples at the Sea of Galilee, Jesus spoke directly to Peter. Yes, He did confront him...not with a question about his cursing and swearing, but with the question, "Do you love me?"

THE PROBLEM OF *TIME* IN UNPACKING HIS SPIRITUAL RUCK

Unfortunately, many warriors don't have time to unpack much. Soon they may face another deployment for which the attitudes, habits, and behaviors that are out of place in the civilian world are an essential part of survival. The tough reality is that, with the virtually back-to-back deployments many infantrymen experience, the ruck can get dirtier and harder to face and sort out later.

A Special Operations chaplain friend gives chilling perspective to this with the following words:

"Leave is a double edged sword. It takes two weeks just to get to the point of being able to relax enough. Then it's time to go back. It is a blessing sometimes because at least then you can turn it back on and not deal with what comes out when (finally) you actually do relax.

"This is the reason that I expect the divorce rate in my unit to skyrocket if we ever stop deploying. With shorter more frequent deployments along with too much (training) time away between deployments, many marriages that have significant problems are limping along because they all have a switch that says 'Just make it till the next trip' They kick everything down the road. He never turns it off and neither does she."

In his eloquently written book, *War*, Sebastian Junger reveals a very painful example from his own life of war's cumulative load of emotional and spiritual damage. He says the psychological impact of war is so profoundly crushing that it may overwhelm and bury for years the more subtle feelings, such as sorrow or remorse, only to release them in an overwhelming flood at some later time.

On an earlier assignment in Liberia, he had seen a lot of dead and wounded people being carried by various makeshift means, and *his emotional reaction* at the time had been *"absolutely zero"*...perhaps because of the terror that reigned around him or because of how "amped" he was by the magnitude of the story he was covering. Then one day, years later, in Paris, he happened to notice two men carrying a sagging mattress across the street, and he "went straight into a full-blown panic...triggering a three week backlog of sorrow and shame."

Many of our warriors who return home after repeated combat deployments and begin unpacking their spiritual ruck may see, smell, hear, or touch something that suddenly and unexpectedly launches them into a similarly devastating "backlog of trauma and shame."

In the final chapter of *War*, Junger puts an exclamation point on this accumulation issue — this backlog of sorrow and shame in the warrior's ruck — by telling of a post-deployment conversation with a soldier he'd gotten to know while covering his platoon in Afghanistan. He relates how confusing and stressful even garrison life had been for the soldier when he re-deployed to the States; and then how, after discharge, adjustment to civilian life had been much worse.

The soldier wants to go back into the Army because, "It's as if I'm self destructive..." He says people tell him that now he can be anything he wants to be. His reply is, "If that's true, why can't I be a...civilian and lead a normal... life?"

Junger replies: *"... you got me there, brother. Maybe the ultimate wound is the one that makes you miss the war you got it in."*

If a warrior is **discharged** or **de-activated after a combat deployment,** he's often on his own to unpack, without help, in front of his family. This is forcefully illustrated in Christian Davenport's book, *As You Were, To War And Back With The Blackhawk Battalion Of The Virginia National Guard*.

Davenport describes how some Guard and Reserve warriors come home, not to the halfway-house of garrison life among fellow combat veterans, but directly into crumbling marriages, broken families, lost jobs, financial hardship, and civilian friends who are blind or indifferent to the sacrifices the civilian warriors have made.

No wonder, then, that some warriors feel an overwhelming need to handle traumatic memories and habits by such things as self-endangering behaviors, "self-medicating," or volunteering to return to combat — to the "safety" of the familiar and manageable — where their combat-altered ways of interacting with life "make sense."

5.

Some Stuff *Most* Combatants Will Need to Unpack.

Whether or not the warriors we serve are heavily involved in a lot of bloody fighting, if they've actually been in combat situations, they will likely still be unloading some trauma or stress-induced issues. If we look deeply into their hearts, first seeking to understand and address their emotional responses, then these familiar residual affects of war will also provide pathways to address *underlying spiritual pain*, and build stronger spiritual foundations for the future.

Following are some of the issues we can expect, and prepare ourselves to help them unpack.

ANGER –

This is one item that, when it's exposed, can often be taken out of his emotional and spiritual ruck by the warrior, faced and talked about, without a great sense of danger (*of course this depends on the source and severity.*) Just don't expect it to "clean up and put away" easily or quickly.

Anger is often unhelpfully viewed as *one unified symptom* of Post-Traumatic Stress or Combat Operational Stress. However, it is *a response to some cause, and it can have a variety of sources.* If a friend says, "I have a headache," we know how silly it would be to automatically respond with, "Here's what I always do for my headaches." Did your friend bump his head, or does he have a migraine, or a brain tumor? Similarly, we need to avoid pulling the, "how to deal with anger," bottle off our biblical counseling shelf and trying to force-feed him a dose. As we follow the expressions of anger back to their source, we'll find that some are troublesome but not devastating, and others are deep rooted and overwhelming to the warrior. We begin by listening, learning, and gaining understanding of the source, and then we'll be able to guide the warrior to appropriate emotional and spiritual understanding with which he may gain God-centered perspective and release.

Following are a few examples of sources of residual anger you may discover in your warrior friend. *As we survey these examples it will be edifying to* **ask ourselves two questions:**

1. Would I guide him to the **same biblical texts** *to resolve* **all of these issues?**

2. What is a **true, God-centered perspective** *my warrior friend needs to gain to begin to find release from* **the particular driving force behind his anger?**

Some examples of sources of residual post-combat anger.

- *Personal baggage*–"anger issues" he *carried with him into combat*, where they were then amplified by trauma.

  In his book, *Shadow Of The Sword,* Marine SSGT and Silver Star recipient Jeremiah Workman tells how he came to the Corps out of a broken home with an abusive stepfather who routinely destroyed dissent in the home either physically or verbally. Workman came home from school one day in time to watch as his stepfather put a gun to his dog's head and pulled the trigger. He says he cried for hours, and now asserts, "… My stepfather taught me how to hate."

Now we must consider the addition of Marine Corps boot camp and advanced infantry training to this frame of mind…and be conscious that *this foundation of hate was laid prior to the bloody combat* that then added the loss of some of his infantry brothers to the reservoir of trauma.

If we wish to understand *his* anger, we must comprehend that the spiritual roots of his rage and hatred are older and deeper than the events he recalls from his combat experience.

In other words, a young man *may already be carrying a load of traumatic anger* when he *enters* combat training, and then "graduates" into a combat situation where he witnesses additional merciless acts being perpetrated against — *or by* — his "brothers."

Now, suppose a young man happens to have had a previous home experience like that described by SSGT Workman; and then this young man — as in a separate case reported in print by an infantryman — *witnesses some of his own squad mates entertaining themselves by killing a litter of puppies they've come upon during a patrol.* Think of the amplified rage that would ride home in this young man's emotional and spiritual ruck at the end of his deployment.

This is not generalized "combat operational stress," and our deeper, more personal understanding of its source will better prepare us to lead the warrior to a biblically sound spiritual release, and to a growing peace.

• *"Bad" command decisions* — which may have led to harm or unnecessary danger. We're talking about war here, not a decision like the one that made you miss a lunch appointment with a friend. In combat, bad decisions can lead to the death or serious injury of a "brother." This is a source of anger that *can rarely be resolved by a young warrior within the command and rank structure.* Combat troops — including officers — only dare talk about this source of anger *among themselves*, or rarely, cautiously, to a trusted friend outside the "danger zone" of rank and authority.

A warrior friend adds a still more frustrating and complicating perspective:

"I have heard rangers talk like this about the best and most caring leaders. But they don't know them because they are too high up the chain. But they have to blame someone for the screw ups." He goes on to add: *"A good leader does not blame decisions on higher levels of command. He owns it. I have watched battalion commanders fight against dumb decisions to the point of almost getting fired. And then when they publish the order, you would never know he didn't agree 100%. He took all of the blame."*

Whether the traumatized warrior's *perspective* on blame is perfectly accurate at the moment or not, some decisions do lead to pain and loss. There is obvious potential for confused, frustrated, unresolved anger coming home in the soul of the warrior with this kind of experience.

Although he may not initially say a lot to us about this source of anger, we shouldn't underestimate the power of the feelings. At least two warriors have told me that this has led to barely restrained murderous rage for them. I'm in communication now with a Special Operations warrior — a believer — for whom this issue teetered on the brink of murder while his unit was still in the battle space, because of decisions by others that led to unnecessary death and injury among some of his friends and subordinates. We must be safe listeners and learn how to help the warrior address the issue with spiritual understanding.

• *Bad follower-ship* — The same knife can cut both ways. Sometimes good leaders' best efforts have been destroyed by power-wielding senior-ranking subordinates, leading to frustration and anger...or even to career-damaging command responses. Friends, even some in Special Operations units, have told me that they have been the victims of "shadow commands" that were formed among those under their authority, undermining their effectiveness and that of the unit.

A chaplain friend experienced harm at the hands of his own assistant, who undermined his spiritual leadership and professional rapport during a deployment to such a degree that it may have damaged his career. Although one who has been so deeply traumatized may recover to some degree and find new direction for life and service, *yet he may be dealing with the spiritual issue of abiding anger, and questions about forgiveness for years.*

A warrior friend shared with me the following first-person example of this *kind* of scenario. In this case the leader in the situation, whose authority was undercut, was not a "good" leader. But the behavior of his subordinates was undoubtedly harmful. There was enough anger to go around, and plenty for all to bring home in their ruck.

"We did the same thing to SSgt H., whom you've heard me regard as a coward. Sgt Z…is probably smarter than any of us. When Z. and H. came in conflict, Z. played by the rules of his chain of command obeying orders…he had a smarter, not harder, mentality when it came to building defenses, and he simply had more undisputable courage and common sense when it came to combat tactics. I do not remember him directly contradicting the platoon sergeant, but had he, we all would have followed him. I think H. knew this, but it didn't stop him from telling anyone who'd listen what idiots Z. and the Lieutenant were."

- **Long periods of hyper-vigilance and deadly danger.** This is now a familiar theme. And yet it is made more potent for me by the request of a Marine SGT friend that I *strongly emphasize this source of residual anger.*

No matter how frequently this is written about, it's hard to adequately convey the impact of this awful reality *in the battle space that is saturated with IEDs.*

In his book, *None Left Behind — The 10th Mountain Division And The Triangle Of Death,* Charles Sasser gives substance to this.

He says the soldiers may as well have "…worn targets on their front and back sides…" *Patrols were sure to be hit **every time they went out,** by IEDs, snipers, mortars, and insurgent fighters.* This meant that, for the Americans on Malibu Road, tasked to drive out insurgents and bring peace and stability to the Triangle Of Death, *each day and night brought casualties and death. It was a dreaded accumulation of hyper-vigilant stress and anger.* The character of the platoon began to change. There had been *so much loss of life, so many casualties, that "…a certain grimness set in."* There was a general sense of fatalism. *"The future no longer existed. Life was lived according to the next patrol, the next run on Malibu Road."*

• **Feeling he has been forced by orders or circumstances to take lives when it seemed unnecessary to him.**
The *flame of anger* stemming from this source is fanned by helpless feelings of *guilt, which become imbedded in*

the warrior's soul. The guilt sends the anger in search of an outlet...a place to discharge the feelings of blame.

- *Frustration and tension of dealing with dangerous "non-combatants" or treacherous "allies."*
In his book, *Outlaw Platoon*, author Sean Parnell tells of one period of combat in which deadly mortar attacks were being launched against his platoon in Afghanistan from across the border, within the operating sector of an "ally" country's army.

And then, adding a "what are we doing here anyway" touch, when they returned to their Forward Operating Base and entered through the Afghan National Army side of the base, they found ANA soldiers who had spent the day inside the wire playing dice games and smoking hash.

Naturally, the rage they felt against the *enemy they were not allowed to pursue* was transferred to these wasted ANA soldiers who wouldn't fight for their own country; but this was *only another object upon which they could not* pour out their pent-up wrath.

This example is not about the behavior of these few ANA soldiers. Many others are admired by our soldiers as proven warriors. This is simply about one source of *pent-up of anger*.

• **Unresolved anger with himself for questionable or bad decisions that resulted in harm.**
This is a confusing source of *soul conflict* in the warrior. The decisions or circumstances that haunt him may or may not have been "bad"; *but if it's unclear to him, and he feels angry or critical with himself, then the conflict is not yet resolved.* He may be receiving therapeutic support that can help him arrive at some reasonable justification or "self forgiveness." *However, when he returns home there will remain in his heart the residual questions: Do I need **forgiveness** for the outcome of my decision? **Who** truly has the **right** to forgive or absolve?"*

You and I have the answer for him, drawn from the authority of God's revelation. God alone is judge. Jesus Christ is our only mediator with God. Understanding, and forgiveness if needed, is possible and complete through Christ alone. Our *spirit* and *approach* in conveying this freeing truth must flow out of a genuine understanding of his inner conflict and a true and fitting application of God's Word for his forgiveness or release from blame.

- *The face-to-face contact he's had with true evil in the world, and the desire to destroy it.*

This is another point that two combat-experienced friends, a Marine SGT, and a Marine CPL, have both asked be strongly emphasized. The SGT once emailed me from Iraq, saying, *"I'm choosing to walk point all the time now. I've seen the face of evil and I want to find it and kill it."*

However, if this kind of situation leads to the war *"becoming personal,"* as one infantry officer puts it, then the warrior will need at some point to face and deal with the *spiritual issue of lingering hatred*. Also, I've known warriors who have eventually had to wrestle with the soul conflict of *mixed feelings of self-justification and shame before God, because they know that they also are sinful men*.

A Special Operations chaplain friend says:

"One thing that clouds the issue is that so many people are telling our warriors that they are ok...that in fact they are more than ok. They are the stuff of American mythology. They are treated as the most trusted and righteous who exist in the country... For anyone who has spent any time on the inside we know, in spite of my own bias and loyalty to my service, that it is not

true. It is misplaced trust on a personal level. Not to mention that I look at me every morning in the mirror and I know that short of the mercy of God I am certainly not ok."

Warriors may find it inescapable to hate the evil they clearly see in war; but when they return home their souls may continue to be subject to the anger and hatred they felt even as the "face"of the evil they've witnessed fades.

- **Delayed anger, recalling unfair treatment of infantry "grunts," by rear-echelon troops.**
This may be a "family matter" between soldiers, similar to inter-service rivalry, but it is a commonly expressed source of residual anger. It's also quite a sensitive matter to talk about, because even bringing it up from the viewpoint of the infantryman seems to present a one-sided indictment of support troops. But we have to face the fact that it's sometimes a source of lingering anger, and help the warrior deal with it at a spiritual level.

What are the ingredients of this source of anger? It's not uncommon for both Army and Marine infantry troops to be treated disrespectfully by support troops – also known to infantry grunts as "POGs" {persons other than grunts} or "Fobbits" {troops remaining in Forward

Operating Bases} when the infantry troops come in dirty and exhausted from Combat Outposts or combat operations.

Marine SSGT Jeremiah Workman gives a pithy example of this in his book, *Shadow Of The Sword.*

He describes a day when his platoon had come in from a protracted period of hard urban fighting. The entire platoon (those who were able to return from the fight) were suffering from shrapnel wounds. They had been unable to eat or clean up for days. They climbed out of their vehicles and straggled off to the mess hall, exhausted and silent, to get some real food after days of dwindling MRE supplies.

At the door they're met by a "rear echelon POG," spotless in his pressed cammies. He shouts at them scornfully that they're not coming in the mess hall until they go clean up. Their Lieutenant goes ballistic and sends the POG away in full retreat. Inside they sit together, still bleeding into their cammies, and when they get up, they leave blood spatters on the deck beneath the tables.

Even my Special Operations chaplain friend says, "*I did the exact same thing with my boys in Iraq after rolling back in after five days of fighting. I felt bad later for taking it out on some junior enlisted (POG) who was just doing her job...but not that bad.'*

Every Infantryman knows that support troops are his lifeline, and this kind of event *does not cause a deep level of trauma*. But this battlefield disconnect can leave some lasting anger that must eventually be resolved, and once it's identified we can help him pull it out of his spiritual ruck, clean it up and put it away.

• *Complex and confusing combinations of events* – (this is one thing that war is *good* at providing.)
Speaking with my Navy Field Corpsman (medic) friend after his two combat tours with Marines in Iraq, we got on this subject of sources of anger among combat troops, such as leadership issues. This led him to tell me a couple of combat stories which, when brought together, help reveal how complex the sources of post-combat anger, stress, and anxiety may be. The first story had to do with a transformation a Marine leader had undergone during combat.

In one targeted operation, the Marine — a man who had already courageously served two previous tours in Iraq, who had children at home, including twin girls — had acted strangely, in what *appeared* to be a cowardly way.

*But then my Corpsman friend recalled an earlier oper-
ation that had probably changed the Marine forever.*

This leader's scouts and my Corpsman friend had
gone into a city ahead of the infantry and LAVs (Light
Armored Vehicles.) They were providing over-watch
security from an elevated position as the infantry came
into the area and began clearing houses. As they entered
to clear a particular house, insurgents ran out the back,
and the infantrymen found a family inside on the floor,
terrified, with hands raised.

The Marine leader referred to above interviewed the
family for intel and then he and his unit went outside
to the front of the house.

*At this point the insurgents came back into the house
from the back, and then fired on a newly arriving Marine
unit in LAVs.* This unit returned fire with the LAV's
powerful guns. Shortly afterward, the man of the house,
whom the Marine leader had just interviewed, came out
with his dead twelve-year-old girl in his arms.

As this part of the story unfolded, my Corpsman friend
and I both realized that the crushing intimacy of this
experience had undoubtedly changed the Marine forever — not out of cowardice or fear for himself, but out

of overwhelming identification with the Iraqi man who had just lost his little girl.

It's not hard to imagine how the trauma of this complex combination of experiences may suddenly and surprisingly surface in the form of anger or possibly extreme anxiety at some post-deployment time when he feels some danger to himself or his children. If we were to look only *superficially* at his anger or anxiety, we couldn't possibly realize the complex source. And this lack of in-depth understanding would not lead to meaningful help for the warrior. With time, compassion, and patience, we must *strive* to *hear* and to truly *know* the warrior and the source of his anger, to meaningfully minister to him.

A fellow Cadence missionary, with experience as a combat leader in Iraq, shares an illustration to help us grasp *the sudden acceleration of severe post-traumatic anger.* He describes it as if a person's emotions are contained in a four-story building.

He sees "normal" anger (that which is not related to combat operations) "residing" on the first and second floor in any person. This anger may occasionally rise to the third floor (rage)...rarely to the fourth (out-of-control rage)

He suggests that *severe* post-traumatic anger *resides on the third floor,* not always visible, but hair-triggered. It exists there as a barely contained raging flame. When this anger is

79

triggered, the raging flame is suddenly revealed, and the anger may roar up to the top floor where murderous thoughts and actions occur that are in touch with the training and execution of war that he has experienced. At this point he may actually, without any conscious intent or hostility to those in his presence, be experiencing feelings of unfocused murderous rage.

Anger can be among the *most*, and the *least*, troublesome issues residing in the warrior's spiritual ruck, depending on its source and nature.

Not everyone who serves in a hostile area experiences the most severe degrees of anger described above. Some of the sources of anger described are *not* of a nature that would lead to *severe* post-traumatic symptoms at all. Some of them, such as the mistreatment of grunts by "POGs," may initially be felt strongly, but after a few months or years only bring a wry smile or a disdainful comment. There are even unit pride issues mixed up in all this that, unlike severe sources of anger, will lose their power when the warrior leaves active duty. Also, I believe that less severe events like these may sometimes actually serve as *outlets — safe pressure releases — for more severe or generalized anger*. All the more reason why we need to *listen and know* our warrior, to meaningfully minister to him.

When *strong, resilient* anger exists and is exposed, spiritual care will begin with walking through the event(s) with the warrior, helping him discover and identify the source of the anger, and then defusing it at its source *primarily by listening compassionately — even repeatedly, if necessary —* and then asking God to grant the supernatural peace that He can supply.

I haven't had the opportunity to study the art of Explosive Ordinance Disposal, but having sometimes observed the thoughtful, delicate work of the EOD tech, I wonder whether it might serve as an illustration of how we should begin to approach the latent explosiveness of the traumatized warrior. We should recognize first that *the "bomb" is not the bomber.* This state he's in was not his plan or desire. It *happened to him.* Although he may be potentially explosive, his anger is a *symptom* of the residual trauma he's experiencing.

We all experience anger. We might wake up in the morning feeling angry with no clue how we got that way. We might come home from work angry over something that was said to us. We might be angry over having been demeaned and humiliated by some abusive treatment we experienced in a store or in traffic. To be real with our warrior friend, we need to ask ourselves, *"What do I do with my anger?"* How do *I* respond when someone says, "What's wrong with you today? Why don't you snap out of it?" *What* and *who* can help *me* at times like these? We need to *be that person* to our warrior friend, with a profound awareness of the source and severity of his residual anger.

The Word of God is replete with references to anger, both God's anger and man's. Anger is assumed in scripture to take place, not condemned for its existence. Interestingly, God doesn't give much instruction about *how to deal with it.*

He warns us against "outbursts" (Galatians 5:20); cautions against letting it lead to sin (Ephesians 4:26); urges us to put it aside (Colossians 3:8); and assures us that our anger does not achieve God's righteousness (James 1:20.)

It seems that the *handling of anger* is what God focuses on in His Word, and He doesn't tell us *how* to handle it in each situation. He apparently leaves it to the Spirit-guided members of the Body of Christ to address it, first in ourselves, and then to assist our brothers and sisters who are having trouble handling it on their own. Perhaps Hebrews 10:22-24 is most applicable. If we *draw near to God with sincere hearts, in full assurance of faith, having our hearts sprinkled clean from an evil conscience and our bodies washed with pure water, and we hold fast the confession of our hope without wavering...* then we will be able to *wisely* **consider how to stimulate our warrior friend to love and good deeds**, which is the *best positive antidote to tenacious anger.*

ABRUPT PERSONAL INTERACTIONS

Like anger, this can be carefully taken out of the emotional battle ruck, looked at and talked about. As with anger, it may not clean up and put away easily, but it's usually a combat "habit," rather than the result of deep trauma. With time, patient understanding, and love it will fade...*unless the warrior is preparing for another combat deployment soon. In that case, he'll need it again and he won't work as hard at cleaning it up as those close to him wish he would.*

82

This may be the part of his spiritual ruck that the returned warrior is least aware of, and the most frustrating to family and friends.

A Marine CPL friend had returned from combat in Iraq and was sitting with me in *The Anchor* servicemen's center in Oceanside, CA, when he received a call on his cell phone. His side of the call was just a few words, all monosyllables, and he didn't initiate any part of the conversation. I figured he was responding to suggestions from a Marine buddy for contact later that day, and I asked him if that was the case. He casually informed me that, no, that had been his fiancé! He took it well when I suggested we work on his comms with people other than grunts.

Family and friends probably don't understand why this kind of communication is in his ruck at all, especially if their warrior doesn't have bloody stories to tell. It probably seems to them that it's something he simply needs to "get over." But this form of interaction plays a very positive and important role in the hostile world he's been living (surviving) in, and may soon return to.

If we haven't been involved in intense combat there's no way we can adequately comprehend the chaotic urgency of communication between elements of a unit in a fight. The platoon and squad leaders may be simultaneously fighting, rushing among their men to provide leadership and encouragement, communicating with leaders above them, and overseeing the effort to get air support. They may be communicating via two, or even three radios at a time for contact with the various elements of their squad, platoon, company, battalion and air.

In this context, the soldier doesn't begin a message with pleasantries, or by excusing himself to the man on the other end for his abruptness and lack of courtesy!

Of course, there's also the detail that he is intensively *trained* in this form of communication for the obvious necessity of it in combat. If this intense form of communication continues for a significant part of his deployment, how could he reasonably be expected to suddenly "get over it"?

Impatience is a familiar part of this abruptness. In the mind of the warrior there is no longer any time or place for delay or trivial things. His training and combat experience demand, "Get on with the mission," and to his war-trained mind, at this point, most things civilians engage in *seem* trivial.

In his book, *War,* Sebastian Junger helps us understand this by pointing out that *warriors often miss combat when they return home.* But it's not getting shot at that they miss; *it's having lived in a world where "everything is important and nothing is taken for granted."* What matters ultimately is whether you can trust one another with your lives. *Anything that is of no consequence in a firefight is of no consequence, period.*

Here's another example, brief and pointed, of how this can manifest itself, post-deployment:

After a combat deployment with the 82nd Airborne Infantry, a chaplain friend counseling West Point cadets told me that he found it difficult to sympathize with a cadet crying on his shoulder over getting a "B" instead of an "A" in a course. My friend completed several other tours to Afghanistan with the 75ᵗʰ Ranger Regiment, where he still serves, and I know that his impatience with triviality has not diminished Impatience, *manifested as abruptness*, may be one of the "war habits" now most deeply embedded in the warrior's character. In this case, at some level, it may be family and friends who need to practice special patience and understanding until their warrior's involvement in the war is over and he can begin his final unpacking process. They'll need spiritual support and guidance with this, and if we are truly and understandingly engaged with them and their warrior, we can help them work through it.

Some thoughts for loved ones and caregivers on how to persevere and be effective in caring for your warrior friend:

- *Ask God* for understanding and patience.
- Do some of the *kind* of *reading* that will give you a taste of the warrior's life in combat and provide some empathy — or at least sympathy. This is one of the reasons I've provided a book list, and not just a bibliography at the end. If you don't get a taste of his combat life, your efforts at patience and understanding will be less effective because the very thing you're trying to deal with remains a blank page for you in his story.

85

- Family members and loved ones, give him some gentle feedback when his words are hard or painful. *Try to help him see **that it's the person you love and miss that's being hidden from you** by harsh words, or the absence of words from him.*

- *Listen for the love beneath his brief words*, and look for it in situations where he doesn't feel pressured and he slows down a bit in his communication. He *is* your friend or loved one, and he *will* be trying.

- *Try not to cause him pressure* by your need or desire for more gentle communication. Pressure will only trigger the thing you're trying to overcome.

- Welcome the more tender communication when it comes and bless him for it...without making the blessing sound like, "See, that's how you're supposed to be."

- *Remind yourself* that by the grace of God this will all change when his deployments are finished.

ANXIETY

Although PTSD is considered an "anxiety disorder," this emotion is not always so severe as to warrant the "disorder" label. However, it can be subtly present, lurking quietly in the returned warrior's spiritual battle ruck and causing hidden damage. It can trigger a surge in any of the other common "items" we find the warrior dealing with as he unpacks. It's also one he'll feel more ashamed of than, for example, anger, because of its implied connection to fear. It may remain hidden behind other, more noticeable issues for some time, while it quietly contributes to discouragement, self-doubt and insecurity.

I have my brother's permission to illustrate this by his post-trauma, post-hyper-vigilance, experience that we walked through together.

Steve was a career cop in a drug-and-crime-infested area in Southern California. He was a lieutenant who had, in addition to various types of undercover work, commanded both the SWAT division and the Career Criminal Division. For some time after he retired, Steve was surprised and puzzled to find himself experiencing anxiety that sometimes escalated to the level of a "panic attack."

I finally gained some helpful insight through a road trip event he experienced and told me about. Driving along normally on the highway, he was suddenly cut off by a car driven recklessly by a lady who then lost control and spun off the road. Thankfully, the car didn't roll over, and Steve quickly stopped to render assistance. All went well, and Steve continued his journey.

This took place some time before I learned much about the effects of combat operations, but the Lord seemed to prompt me to ask him the question, "How were you feeling during this event?" Today, reflecting on his answer, it's simply understandable, but at the time it was as if a light came on for me when Steve replied, "I felt perfectly calm."

Crisis had been his "normal" state for so many years that, since his retirement, his body and mind had been anxiously waiting to feel normal again…perhaps over-responding to the faintest signals of danger, only to be left "holding the bag" of body-produced action drugs with no way to use them. What Steve was experiencing is one of the things we find many of our warriors dealing with when they return home.

I've read that during the Vietnam War, the military conducted studies of cortisol levels in carrier pilots and Special Forces soldiers, related to danger and anticipated danger. Cortisol is a steroid hormone produced by the adrenal gland. This is referred to in Junger's book, *War,* and the studies illustrate the practical effects of anxiety from the experience of a Special Forces team in Vietnam.

It is reported that the cortisol levels of the soldiers *dropped* — they felt *less* anxious — as an anticipated attack drew near; but then began to *rise* when the attack did not materialize. The soldiers' psychological defenses had developed to such an extent that an expected attack actually created a *positive* feeling of readiness, a feeling of euphoric expectancy. The soldiers were more at ease facing a known threat than anxiously waiting for an unknown possibility. And so, as in my brother's situation, the *byproduct* of this amazing mental-biological preparation system God has built into us is the *hidden follow-up effect* that warriors experience — *persistent anxiety*…waiting…watching, for the "inevitable" attack.

Anxiety is a *"sneaky"* thing in each of our lives, and the post-combat warrior is no exception. In his case it is aggravated by its hated insinuation of fear. It is like a living thing, creeping around in his emotional and spiritual ruck, *denying its own presence*, while *nagging at him over every appearance of weakness or failure* and *suggesting threats* at everything that reminds him of combat.

Physicians prescribe anti-anxiety drugs for warriors experiencing these symptoms, but this is not intended as a long-term solution and *personal* emotional and spiritual care is needed. Ongoing interpersonal involvement and loving collaboration are required if the warrior is to get hold of this slippery thing, look it in the eye, and begin the process of "throwing it over" onto Christ. 1 Peter 5:7. As my Marine CPL friend expressed to me:

"When we were released from active duty we were given phone numbers, business cards and encouragement to contact mental health professionals. None of us used any of it. I only talked to you and my family, because you had gone through so much with me and you understand."

Anxiety, like pain and fear, has its useful function as a warning that something needs attention. Also, like pain and fear, it can become consuming and *seem to be* the main issue. The solution to pain and fear is in *counteracting* the cause. But with anxiety, which is nebulous and not necessarily attached to a real present threat, the solution is learning to ***trust…to rest in a guardianship that never sleeps***, *while looking the anxiety in the eye and regaining perspective.*

*The difficult questions for the warrior, who has been intensely, personally **responsible** for issues of life and death, are: to trust in **what**, or **whom** outside of himself? And **how to learn** to trust.*

To simply come alongside the warrior and exhort him not to be anxious, would probably elicit, *as it would with any of us*, a denial of anxiety or an irritated, "If I knew how to do that I would have done it already!" He will need the support and guidance of specific words from God. But first he needs an *envoy* from God — a *friend* who has earned his trust by non-judgmentally listening to his experiences and graciously *probing the information* he shares for the emotional and spiritual *load* related to it. This is not merely to acknowledge his feelings, but to *feel the load on your own shoulders with him, to see and understand how it is that anxiety still lingers over events that are no longer present threats. **From this position, with our own shoulder under his load,*** we are better able to recall and share words from God that are releasing and healing. Proverbs 12:25 says, "Anxiety in a man's heart weighs it down, but a good word makes it glad." "Good" words are those that are God-inspired, encouraging, timely, and welcome.

If your warrior friend knows he's loved, and he senses your shoulder alongside his own under the load of anxiety he's bearing, then he will welcome your offer to *pray together with him* for the assurance of God's promise in Philippians 4:6-7 —

"Be anxious for nothing, but in everything by prayer and supplication with thanksgiving let your requests be made known to God. And the peace of God, which surpasses all comprehension, will guard your hearts and your minds in Christ Jesus."

This, then, will not be received as an "outsider's" thoughtless exhortation, but as a partner helping bear his load. The most important thing is not that his load feels lighter for the moment, but that God will answer your prayers of faith. You are *helping him begin to trust God* for the surpassing peace he needs, and the guarding of his heart and mind, which are the specific needs of his anxious heart. But hold on...now is not the time to heave a sigh of relief and walk away, pleased that such a heavy emotional task is behind you. The partnership has just begun, and anxiety is sneaky.

FORCEFULNESS

Before his combat training and deployment he was a smiling, patient, easy-going friend, son, husband, or dad.

Now the smile is grim and forced. Everything he says seems to be spoken in the form of an order, as if it's a life-or-death issue. This is because so many things *are*, in the world he has come home from.

A true, understanding friend — not a "stranger" — can help him unpack this piece, not by arguing with him over the content of his command, or rebuking him for it ("You shouldn't have said that to your little sister."). But by a loving and timely arm around the shoulder and gracious reminder of "where he is." Over time I've watched as warriors have come to realize that home is not the battle space, and have begun to lighten up. This storm will pass; and with patience and understanding, family and friends can weather it.

However, again, if he is set for back-to-back deployments, this too is a piece of "equipment" that will have to remain ready in his ruck. To some degree his family and friends will have to continue to understand, bear up, and adapt until the war is over for their warrior. They'll need godly, understanding, patient, *present* support by Christian friends, chaplain, or pastor to persevere without wavering in this loving struggle as it is prolonged. And nothing helps the warrior more than those characteristics in his family and friends.

ISOLATION

Spareness of speech. Compressed lips. Distant look when asked questions. "Disappearance," that is, retreat into private activities, removed from family and friends.

These symptoms may be the result of:

- His mind *churning with things that need to be said*, but not *daring* to say *anything.*
- Not knowing *what* can be said *safely.*
- Not being able to *organize a thought* out of the chaos war has made of his mind.
- Not finding anything in civilian conversations *worthy of speaking to,* compared to the memories and images that fill his thoughts.
- Not being able to think of anything to share *that you could possibly understand.*
- *Unwillingness to expose himself* to ignorant, or even judgmental comments.
- *The impossibility of responding to questions at every new contact with individuals or groups.* It's easier to avoid contact with people than to try to figure out how to answer even the simplest and most sincere questions every time he bumps into an acquaintance at church or in a store. He's often thinking, "How can I answer a sincere, 'How are you doing?' when I *don't even know* how I'm doing? And, how much of the answer do you really want to hear? Are you ready to hear how I'm *really* doing right at this moment…this moment when I just happen to be wishing I was back with my squad in combat where life is 'less complicated and confusing?' You might be happy just to hear me say, 'I'm doing okay,' but a lot of the time that would be a lie."

93

This kind of isolation is *not* arrogance or indifference. *It's more akin to hopelessness, and it is a lonely place to live.* (Emphasis urged by a Marine SGT friend.)

Help in addressing this symptom of hidden pain involves love, patience, undemanding attitude, readiness-to-listen, and preparing yourself not to be easily offended or shocked. *What's in there is in there!* When he takes the risk of stepping out of his isolation and something ugly is exposed, we don't want to be the reason he throws it back in the bag and slips back into his isolation.

Not long ago, God enabled a renewed contact for me with a Marine who was especially close to us during his combat deployments in Iraq in 2004-05. Following his deployments, he had told me — among other things — that killing was a rush, and he had killed people until the rush wore off. A short time later he turned his back on us and on the Lord...the result of severe symptoms of PTSD, the most prominent of which was consciousness of *spiritual guilt*.

Later, he began to talk to me again by phone, and began opening himself even more deeply than before. Honestly, the things he started sharing are painful for me to hear, and not repeatable here. He is one of those who have said to me, "You don't understand, I was a bad person in combat!" But he was talking to me again, and allowing me to talk to him about God. I prayed, "Lord help me...I don't want to be the cause of his throwing his spiritual ruck back in some dark place," and re-isolating himself.

The main point, speaking of this matter of *isolation*, is that most of these young warriors *cannot* articulate the pain, sadness, and horror they've seen and participated in.

Furthermore, they know that if they could express it, we couldn't grasp it.

Yet more tragically, they know that in most cases we wouldn't care enough to suffer through the hearing of it.

Thankfully, there *are some* men and women — such as recovering warriors who *want to talk it through in print*, and embedded war correspondents — who have suffered the horrors of war and *are* able (eventually) *to articulate it on behalf of the warriors.*

One of the most articulate among these is Dexter Filkins, correspondent and author. He has been embedded with our warriors in both Iraq and Afghanistan. Among his powerful books is, *The Forever War.*

He speaks of the naïve hunger his readership had for the material he sent back from the battle space…and then of what it was like to be *"…back in the world…floating…through the regular people in the regular world."*

He reflects on the seriousness of people's feelings about such important things as sandwich fillings and ballgame scores. And he tells how the war has flattened and deadened emotional existence for him. There had been so many bombs, so many screams, that it now all seemed to happen silently and in slow motion. And now, back in "the world," everything seems the same — slow and heavy and dead.

He says when you come home your days die, but your dreams explode. And he believes that most of the grunts he knew seemed the same, "...floating...among the normals."

It's not our spiritual responsibility to try to "fix" our isolated warrior friend, but **to *try to go and find him in that silently screaming place where he lives*; and *by God's grace walk with him through that dark valley until he finds light and peace.***

If he lets me in and I "find him" in that dark place, then what does he need from me? What can I bring to him for his journey toward light and peace?

- First, *my quiet, peaceful presence*. In a simpler context I have *felt* the power of this myself. At one time in my ministry life I found myself mentally and spiritually exhausted and I was walking alone in the woods near my home when I saw a close friend approaching. The last thing I wanted at the moment was to try to carry on a conversation. The Lord, Himself, must have brought my friend to me at that moment, for he fell in beside me and walked quietly with me, without uttering a word or asking a question. It felt as if he took up part of my load and carried it with me. That was over forty years ago, and the power of his ministry of silent, peaceful presence is fresh in my heart today.

- *Assurance of God's ability to bring him safely through the valley.* If your warrior friend is a believer, Psalm 23 is

God-breathed assurance of hope and deliverance. He may be willing to read it and meditate on it; and you can be the voice of God, reminding him that this is meant for him.

• An *"interpreter"* of the truth of God regarding his memories and feelings. This is a *key ministry*, but it's the most difficult part, because:

o It requires the warrior to trust you enough to *explore and expose his memories* and share the most painful ones with you. He will not...cannot...do this with more than one or two trusted friends.

o It requires you to partake of his painful memories, and to do the *hard labor of prayerfully searching out restorative truth in God's Word according to what he shares*. He might be mutely suffering the effects of one overwhelmingly evil event he's witnessed, or some wicked thing he himself has done. Or he might be struggling to find a workable perspective on the whole massive wickedness of the war he's been immersed in. It's impossible to prepare a list of applicable scriptures here for every possible issue he may reveal. In fact, that would lead to the counterproductive behavior of "checking boxes." We each need to plead with God for understanding, and for His guidance to find the peace-imparting truth that will lead the warrior out of the darkness he's taken refuge in. However, God has said some foundational things we can freely share with him. Your warrior friend has sought refuge in his isolation, but God assures him in that He Himself is a trustworthy refuge to turn to in the most confusing and frightening times:

"God is our refuge and strength, a very present help in trouble. Therefore we will not fear, though the earth should change and though the mountains slip into the heart of the sea;" Psalm 46:1-2

God assures him that He has *felt* his loneliness and rejection:

"He was despised and forsaken of men, a man of sorrows and acquainted with grief; and like one from whom men hide their face He was despised, and we did not esteem Him." Isaiah 53:3

"… He Himself has said, 'I WILL NEVER DESERT YOU, NOR WILL I EVER FORSAKE YOU,' so that we confidently say, 'THE LORD IS MY HELPER, I WILL NOT BE AFRAID.' What will man do to me?" Heb. 13:5-6

- *A "communications guide."* As God leads him out of the darkness and he begins to be willing to rebuild connections with "normal" people, he still *may not know what to say.* We've already seen that some of the walls of his prison of silence are made up of *not knowing* what *can*, or *should*, be said. What can I say safely? What does the average person in my life need, or have a right, to know? What am I *supposed* to say if I want to be socially functional again? How do I reply to curious people? How much truth do I need to share in reply to simple questions? These questions are a daily, moment-to-moment interpretive obstacle to your recovering warrior friend because he'll waver between feeling guilty, angry, puzzled, offended, and frustrated. He needs a little confident support and guidance in this, and the *assurance of freedom* to calmly say as little as he feels is appropriate in any situation.

6.

THE SOUL AT WAR

This section is about trying to grow in our understanding of *what's taking place in the soul* of the warrior, and an exploration of what helps heal and restore his traumatized soul following combat. We'll look through the lenses of physical and emotional trauma, into *the impact of war on his relationship to the God of the Bible*.

Below are passages, quotations, and thoughts that represent some of my own purposeful exploration into a *biblical understanding* of war-induced *soul conflict* and how to help bring spiritual healing to our damaged warriors. Hopefully by this means we will move beyond merely repeating the familiar texts that most warriors have often heard preached, and to which many have become desensitized. It is my prayer that the caregivers who read these words will be launched into searching out even wiser, deeper and more effective biblical understanding.

Some of these passages and thoughts are directed *to the warrior* for his help, and some *to the one who would help*, through the application of the Words of God.

━━━━◆◆◆━━━━

Hebrews 9:6-14 – is, I think, a key passage in addressing this painful reality with the warrior. Referring to Levitical "regulations of divine worship," the writer says:

*"Now when these things have been so prepared, the priests are continually entering the outer tabernacle performing the divine worship, but into the second, only the high priest enters once a year, not without taking blood, which he offers for himself and for the sins of the people committed in ignorance. The Holy Spirit is signifying this, that the way into the holy place has not yet been disclosed while the outer tabernacle is still standing, which is a symbol for the present time. **Accordingly both gifts and sacrifices are offered which cannot make the worshiper perfect in conscience, since they relate only to food and drink and various washings, regulations for the body imposed until a time of reformation.** But when Christ appeared as a high priest of the good things to come, He entered through the greater and more perfect tabernacle, not made with hands, that is to say, not of this creation; and not through the blood of goats and calves, but through His own blood, He entered*

the holy place once for all, having obtained eternal redemption. For if the blood of goats and bulls and the ashes of a heifer sprinkling those who have been defiled sanctify for the cleansing of the flesh, how much more will the blood of Christ, who through the eternal Spirit offered Himself without blemish to God, cleanse your conscience from dead works to serve the living God?"

The "external" helps we offer, such as medical treatment, psychological guidance, calming exercises, self-forgiveness, resilience training, decorations and awards, and peer-level discussion groups, like the "gifts and sacrifices" of verse 9 do achieve their fitting work. But they are temporal. *The spiritual work of "reformation" is needed for the cleansing of the conscience and freedom of the soul. Verse 10*

Verse 9 says that this is because these *"cannot make the worshiper (or the internally struggling warrior) perfect in conscience."*

He may be involved in a *hidden moral battle* — perhaps wrestling with awareness of some evil he knows he has committed, or questions of *"sins committed in ignorance" in war.* Verse 7 This is true of many of our warriors, and the *limitations of the "external" helps* leave them alone to fight their internal war. One combat-embedded author gives an example of how this can take place in the warrior. He says that most firefights go by so fast that acts of bravery or cowardice are essentially spontaneous. A soldier might find himself in lifelong regret of a decision he doesn't even remember making.

Even the passage of time doesn't necessarily heal wounds and questions of conscience. Sometimes it only deepens the warrior's sense of hopelessness. I have the permission of my brother (not the police officer) to share the following thoughts. Rick fought through two tours in Vietnam in the Navy's Riverine Force in the Mekong delta and Danang. He came home with a purple heart and two Bronze Stars, both with combat 'V' for valor, and several other medals.

For years he never uttered a word about his service. He didn't get the PTSD *label*, which hadn't yet come into use, but he got the whole emotional and spiritual load. He tried to deal with the pain by isolating himself, even from family and friends. One day he might show up for work, and the next day be found in his darkened house, sitting with a blanket over his head.

When, after many years, he finally began to talk to me about the war, the very first event he mentioned was the first of many times his boat was ambushed from the surrounding jungle. He returned fire with the boat's .50 caliber and watched as a uniformed VC soldier was cut in two by his fire. After the firefight, as they were assessing the situation ashore, he found the soldier, who turned out to be a child of about fourteen years of age.

This had been his first firefight. It had happened many years ago. And yet it was the first memory that sprang to his mind.

However effective our temporal support may be, *spiritual wounds remain*, and the passage of time may only drive them deeper into the trenches of the soul, making it a longer, harder battle for the warrior to be set free from the painful memories and questions. Even the recalling and telling of these inner wounds does not set one free. *This requires a spiritual process — the work of the Spirit of God to purge the conscience of imagined or real defilement and to grant assurance that the soul is clean before God, which is the foundation for the soul's healing and restoration.*

Rick found peace with God through a cleansed conscience. He went on to become a pastor and has served several churches. Yet even today *the residue of pain and sadness lingers at various levels*. He still values ongoing counseling support, and still experiences nightmares and flashbacks, in which he re-lives the smells, sounds and terror of the events.

Rick's situation highlights the need for the spiritual "re-formation" of the conscience and ultimately of the body's natural residual responses referred to in verse 10. This comes through the *continuing ministry* of the Holy Spirit within the warrior who has received the assurance of Christ's unblemished sacrifice. Verse 14 Rick's conscience is free, but the re-formation of his *body's memories* is still underway. He tells me that nightmares are less frequent now, but they, as well as the flashbacks ("re-experiencing"), are still overpowering at times.

Each warrior soul has been immersed in an environment that generates moral abhorrence and conflicted thoughts and feelings. The point is to help the warrior ***address*** the spiritual confusion — the *soul damage of real or perceived "defilement."* One who has gone to war *without* the knowledge of God will especially need the truth of this passage.

Hebrews 10:19-23 –- assures us that we can confidently enter the holy place — the presence of God — through the blood of Christ. We can draw near with a sincere heart in full assurance of faith, having our ***hearts*** *sprinkled clean from an evil conscience* and our ***bodies*** *washed with pure water;* and we can *keep our hope* without wavering ***because He who promised is faithful.*** It is not the warrior's worthiness or reliability, but *God's faithfulness to His promise*, which is his hope and assurance.

Officially credentialed caregivers are allowed — even encouraged, these days — to address the "spirituality" of the warrior. In fact, *it is considered to be one of the pillars of resilience in the life of the combatant.* But, *spirituality* remains a nebulous term, open to interpretation and application by any caregiver. It is not the responsibility of medical and psychological caregivers to counsel the warrior — as in Hebrews 9 and 10 — that the blood of Christ is the one-and-only cleanser of the conscience.

The author of some of the most helpful psychological resources I've read is — I think — a believer. She writes an entire chapter in one of her books on how "souls" become casualties of war. However, undoubtedly to have her books approved for general use by the military, she governs her language by saying that she does not refer to the soul in a "religious way." So in her books she addresses the warrior's spirituality from the usual secular perspective. This is not to diminish the quality of her psychological care; but simply to acknowledge that it does not address the warrior soul's relationship to God.

In our military the parameters of both psychological and spiritual counsel are set by the constraints of pluralism, and "proselytizing" is not permitted.This introduces a difficult point for caregivers within the community who believe the Bible's declaration that it is *Christ alone and His unique sacrifice that cleanses and heals the wounded conscience; and the Apostle Paul's words, "There is one God and one Mediator between God and men the Man Christ Jesus."* 1 Timothy 2:5 In the secularly defined form of pluralism we have in America today, any suggestion that another viewpoint may be less true than our own, or attempt to persuade another to reject any false hope and trust in Christ alone, is viewed as intolerance, and amounts to coercion. In the context of military rank and authority, the complexity of this is amplified for the spiritual caregiver.

To truly serve him, we must *know* our warrior friend *in all the dimensions of his post-combat life, and minister to him according to his experience and need.* The *souls* of traumatized warriors are at stake, not only their physical bodies and emotional state. *It is only the blood of Christ that cleanses the **conscience** and the '**body'** — the outer man whose senses replay the destructive memories. The mind begins to be set free from this destructive treadmill of memories and fears when the conscience has been cleansed and the soul set free.*

In Romans 8:11 Paul promises that, "...if the Spirit of Him Who raised Christ Jesus from the dead dwells in you, *He who raised Christ Jesus from the dead **will also give life to your mortal bodies through His Spirit who dwells in you.***" *This is the revitalization warriors need for their confused, guilt-ridden, angry, disoriented mortal minds and bodies.*

In **Proverbs 3:19-26**, vs. **26** says, *"For the Lord will be your confidence..."* In this proverb, Solomon urges us to *"**keep sound wisdom and discretion**" that they may be "**life to your soul** and adornment to your neck..**then you will walk in your way securely and your foot will not stumble**. When you lie down your sleep will be sweet. Do not be afraid of sudden fear nor of the onslaught of the wicked when it comes; for the Lord will be your confidence and will keep your foot from being caught."* This is a promise of **spiritual** security that he refers to, not that the warrior will never fear or lose sleep in combat!

Being proverbial, this passage may speak of any "onslaught" one may face and certainly war is one of the worst. It does not necessarily refer to the human enemy as "the wicked," although they may be so. *But the effects of the onslaught of combat on the human soul are certainly wicked.*

In helping the warriors God brings under our care to **prepare** for the "sudden fear" of this onslaught — whether for their first deployment or for a return to the known horror — *we must try to help them understand that there is a **spiritual confidence** that may be theirs. It is the **result of finding and keeping sound wisdom and discretion…in the knowledge of God Himself.** Then, whatever form the onslaught takes, **God Himself** will be the warrior's confidence.

Chaplain Mike Hoyt shares the following thoughts (revised a bit with his permission for use here.)

"The inner wounds are a result of trauma. The human soul can only endure so much abuse. God set limits to our humanity to keep us human. When those limits are transgressed, we suffer injury to our humanity (our God-given conscience) and sense of right and wrong, and become traumatized. The circumstances that created the trauma are independent of the inner feeling results. When we deal with scriptures that talk about confidence in God, we deal with the fundamentals of faith that establish the relationship with God, which engenders confidence at some stage

of growing in grace. (It would not be appropriate to label war-damaged souls) as "lacking confidence in God" or not being faithful enough to overcome the horror. God transforms our life through the exercise of faith, not at the exclusion or denial of what has happened to us, but knowing full well the mess, and reconciling it to Himself. God makes living with the horror possible. Jesus is resurrected with the nail holes and spear thrust. We must teach others in authentic faith to live with their horrors, assured that Christ rescues, transforms, and reconciles our deepest wounds to His glory."

It's important, especially with young combatants, to help them understand that this is not an automatic or magical provision, but rather *the result of pursuing and keeping the knowledge of the One Who founded the earth and established the heavens.* 1 John 2:24, 25, 28. Most warriors know *about* God. Our task is to assist them in coming to *know Him* and to *keep* His sound wisdom and discretion.

Almost all infantrymen I've met and worked with are taught by their leaders to memorize and refer to Psalm 91 before going into battle. They are urged to claim for themselves the powerfully worded security of its promises. Those who are believers and followers of Christ can rightly take great confidence and *spiritual security* from this passage. I am burdened with the knowledge, however, that although these promises are for those who according to verse 14 *have loved and known God*, some who are encouraged to lean on the security of the passage are themselves still standing dangerously in the place of "the wicked" of verse 8.

As inspirational as this Psalm feels to anxious troops approaching combat, it is not true or "safe" biblical guidance to apply it generally.

This danger is illustrated in these words from my Special Operations warrior friend:

"I had a commander who was a faithful member of a local church and helped teach Sunday school. But as soon as it was time to speak at a memorial ceremony he turned into a follower of Norse mythology and not a Christian. He spoke about how warriors would gather in a great hall in heaven. Grieving parents would speak about how it gave them comfort. Unfortunately, it was a false hope. Even brave and selfless warriors have to stand before the judgment seat. Just because our culture currently gives us a bye on everything doesn't mean our Creator will do the same."

Warriors really do die in combat and stand before the eternal Judge of all creation. We who care for warriors' *souls* should not offer them false comfort as if it were God's Word to them, but rather provide instruction and guidance that offers true hope.

God says through Jeremiah:

"...Do not listen to the prophets who are prophesying to you...They speak a vision of their own imagination, not from the mouth of the Lord. They keep saying to those who despise Me, 'The Lord has said, "You will have peace"'; And as for everyone who walks in the stubbornness of his own heart, they say, 'Calamity will not come upon you.'...I have heard what the prophets have said who prophesy falsely in My name, saying, 'I had a dream, I had a dream!' (verse 25)...The prophet who has a dream may relate his dream, but let him who has My Word speak My word in truth...declares the Lord."(verse 28) Selections from Jeremiah 23:16-28.

Warriors need true biblical understanding to prepare themselves for the fearful possibilities of war. They need true biblical guidance to address their fears before combat, the traumas resulting from it, and their accountability to God. In our integrity, and in faithfulness to the warrior who faces death, he should at least be instructed in the true meaning of Psalm 91 and given the opportunity to *become* the one who loves the Savior, as in verse 14.

There is another Psalm I would offer him that is relevant and inspirational, *and it is worded in the form of a confession*, which would grant the warrior an *opportunity to consider and believe.*

Preserve me, O God, for I take refuge in you. I said to the LORD, "You are my Lord; I have no good besides you." As for the saints who are in the earth, they are the majestic ones, in whom is all my delight. The sorrows of those who have bartered for another god will be multiplied; I shall not pour out their drink offerings of blood, nor will I take their names upon my lips. The LORD is the portion of my inheritance and my cup; You support my lot. The lines have fallen for me in pleasant places; indeed, my heritage is beautiful to me. I will bless the LORD Who has counseled me; indeed my mind instructs me in the night. I have set the LORD continually before me; because he is at my right hand, I will not be shaken.

Psalm 16:1-8

Adam Brown, a SEAL Team SIX operator whose life is described in Eric Blehm's book, *Fearless,* was living out this psalm before he laid down his life in an operation against a major Taliban leader in Afghanistan. It seems to me that Adam is one warrior who truly understood this Psalm, and its spirit is captured almost line-by-line, in a letter to his wife, found after his death.

His letter was written while lying in bed one night, ready to sleep, but feeling the awareness that something could happen to him in the week of operations that lay ahead. As if reading from Psalm 16, he pours out to his wife and little boy how precious they are to him, how God has blessed him with the life He has chosen for him with them...so blessed that it made his "blood burn with completeness." He reminds his wife that this is the day that the Lord has made, and how deeply he desires that they will always show their boy that Jesus Christ is "the greatest Man on Earth."

He closed his letter with the promise of his love through eternity. And as he usually did, he added a verse of scripture. This night, as his heart instructed him according to God's counsel, he prepared his wife and baby for what lay ahead that they might not to be shaken, because God was at their right hand.

The scripture he left with them was 1 Peter 5:10.

"After you have suffered for a little while the God of all grace, who called you to His eternal glory in Christ, will Himself perfect, confirm, strengthen, and establish you."

My own prayer is, *Oh God, teach us how to help our warriors be as spiritually prepared as Adam was.*

7.

CHRONIC SPIRITUAL CONFLICT IN WARRIORS

Most people who care enough to look are painfully aware of the effects of physical trauma inflicted on those who do our fighting and rescuing for us. Infantrymen, security troops, close support aviators, and field medical staff are particularly in the line of fire, and absorb the main physical force that comes against us. And there are increasing numbers of folks in "non-combat" MOSs experiencing trauma from hostile action.

The skills of today's medical caregivers are marvelous, from the battlefield to the rehabilitation hospitals. And when their efforts are combined with the courage and strength of our wounded warriors, physical recovery is being achieved to an unprecedented degree. The accompanying reality is that there is an increasing number of warriors whose lives and bodies are being saved, but who *remain in a state of spiritual distress.*

LONG-TERM SPIRITUAL HARM

There is damage done **universally** *to the human soul by the conduct of war.*

However, I believe there is an *additional,* ***potentially more lasting dimension of damage*** for those who have actually been required to *engage in killing.*

Those who become our heroes by carrying out *the assignment of violence and killing* in war also receive the unadvertised, *sometimes lifelong,* assignment of dealing with ***chronic*** — *that is, unresolved* — soul damage. I believe this is distinct, not necessarily in its manifestations, but in its ***nature*** and ***duration*** from the harm received in combat by those whose responsibilities do not *require them to directly commit violence and killing.*

I'll briefly insert one preliminary comment in support of this statement. It's evident from the focused discussion on **FORGIVENESS** further down in the book that it is not those who have "received" harm, but those who have *done the violence* who plead, not for thanks, but for forgiveness.

Many warriors spend weeks, months, or even years dealing with the post-traumatic memories of horrors they have witnessed or the ugly realization that, *"someone tried to kill me"*…or that, *"someone destroyed part of my body."*

But there is an additional dimension of soul trauma for one who spends the remainder of his life dealing with the memory that *he took the lives of other human beings and was instrumental in ushering them into their eternal destiny.*

There are illustrations in our civilian experience to help us grasp this difference. For example, one would be severely traumatized if he were badly injured in an automobile accident in which, also, a close friend is killed. But the *driver* of the car, who bears responsibility for the accident, will obviously experience a different kind and degree of emotional and soul harm. He will be forced to deal with the spiritual pain and questions arising out of having been instrumental in ushering another human being into his ultimate destiny.

This distinction further reveals the deeper truth that, although *soul damage* obviously also involves psychological trauma, yet it is **distinct** in that **it is a matter to be addressed between the warrior and God.** He may readily say, "I am not guilty before God for *being hurt in combat.*" But he will need to find the answer to the further question, *"Am I* guilty before God for *hurting and killing others?"* For some warriors this question is *never* adequately dealt with.

In his book, *What It Is Like To Go To War,* Karl Marlantes, decorated combat veteran, makes this simple but profound comment:

"We cannot expect normal eighteen-year-olds to kill someone and contain it in a healthy way."

What I'm calling **chronic** *spiritual conflict* is that which becomes *entrenched* in a warrior's *mind and spirit* as a result of having consciously, deliberately, energetically, and in some cases, viciously, engaged in the horrors and moral abandonment of combat. As I write these words I have just

116

received the message that my own brother, the Vietnam vet I spoke of earlier, is experiencing an earlier than usual onset of the crushing *annual reawakening* of his PTSD symptoms. This usually occurs around Christmas time...this year it has begun in October.

I believe *this form of damage is uniquely destructive and distinct,* even from the most profound and destructive traumas that *happen **to*** the warrior through incoming fires, IEDs, the painful memories that medical people and spiritual caregivers retain, the soul-grinding sadness of seeing young children tortured and raped by insurgents, and numberless other atrocities. My brother would not say that his entrenched, recurring pain is the result of the destruction of his body and loss of most of his teeth through two years of jungle warfare in Vietnam, but that it is the result of the *conduct of war.*

The descriptors used, such as Post-Traumatic Stress Disorder, Combat Operational Stress, and others, *potentially involve* the hidden dimension of **chronic** *spiritual conflict* I'm concerned with here. Crucial help for the warrior comes through skilled medical, cognitive, and behavioral therapies. But it's not the domain of these approaches to address the poison of *chronic soul conflict.* In our care for the warrior, if this distinction is not made he may receive excellent medical and psychological help, and yet be left with the lifelong plea I have already quoted, *"I don't want thanks; I want to be forgiven!"*

By my own observations of warriors moving in and out of combat, pursuing or not pursuing mental health support, finding or not finding competent help, I'm persuaded that the **chronic** *spiritual conflict* in their hearts is rarely addressed adequately, if at all. (I use the word "heart" in the New Testament sense of our deepest personal being, understanding, and belief; e.g., Matthew 15 and Luke 2.)

I believe hidden spiritual conflict often becomes the *chronic poison* that lingers in warriors for many years. I think it can also be a fatal poison if the dose is high enough. That is to say, I suspect it plays a leading, though perhaps unconscious, part in self-endangering or self-punishing behaviors that are commonly attributed primarily to survivor guilt, anxiety, and adrenalin need.

Some of the most experienced, compassionate and practical writers I've read are the authors of the book, *I Always Sit With My Back To The Wall,* Dr. Harry A. Croft, and Rev. Chrys Parker. In the book, they address the reality of the spiritual and make reference to God. However, it is not within their standpoint to address the damage to the *warrior's soul from the perspective* of *biblical authority.* Included in their summary thoughts on s*earching for new sources of spiritual support,* they express gratefulness for our society's many different belief systems and religious communities. If a warrior does not feel supported by past religious affiliations, formed "by default" from family and cultural traditions, he is urged to explore other faith communities that are in harmony with his or her "personal spirituality."

Regrettably, this advice finds the soul-damaged warrior in the *"spiritual paralysis"* referred to further on under the heading of *SPIRITUALITY, convinced that **nobody ultimately really knows** what is true or right.* So the spiritually struggling warrior enjoys the liberty of exploring for healing spiritual truth...but how is he to confidently *recognize* the truth among all the spiritual options? Or is he to assume that *any* spiritual option he settles upon is as useful as any other in resolving his soul's conflict about sin, righteousness and judgment? The restoration of the warrior who is experiencing destructive, chronic soul damage through participation in the acts of killing must begin — not with unguided exploration of various religious traditions — but with *God's Words* addressed to this grinding issue of guilty fear.

There's a biblical example of this in the life and death of John the Baptist. Before the circumstances leading up to John's beheading, Herod had been a powerful warrior. When his warrior life had devolved into that of a dissolute king, his post-war lifestyle of partying and womanizing led to the imprisonment of John. The problem for him was that *John kept preaching **words of Truth**, and Herod kept him safe in his brig because he liked to listen to him. **The Words** fascinated* and captivated him, but rather than *heed* the words, he did what many of our warriors believe they are *supposed* to do... *he kept his spiritual options open.*

Then, "one strategic day," under the influence of a stag party and a girl (are we surprised?), Herod forfeited any future opportunity to hear and respond to God's Words of Life, by taking John's life. Following this, when everyone in Jerusalem was speculating about who Jesus was, *Herod was fixated on his fear that this could only be the resurrected John, whom he had killed*. By now he knew enough about God through John's preaching to be terrorized, *but he was imprisoned in his soul fear*. If only he had **heeded** the **words** of life. *The power of guilty fear in the soul is impenetrable without true understanding of God, and either His reassurance or His forgiveness, which are the only certain hope of restoration for the chronically fearful warrior's soul.*

I believe that, to get in touch with this inner spiritual conflict requires **stepping into the battlefield of the warrior's mind and soul and joining him in the war to reconcile that which seems irreconcilable to him — is, in fact, irreconcilable, apart from assurance from the One Who has ultimate authority over life and death, whether that assurance is the clarification of blamelessness, or the purification of confession and forgiveness.** If there is real guilt, then *forgiveness* — the dismissal or sending away of guilt — is an objective reality that the warrior may receive by the mercy and grace of God through faith in the sacrificial death and resurrection life of Jesus Christ who, Himself, said, *"...any sin and blasphemy shall be forgiven people..."* Matthew 12:31

If the warrior is a believer, he will struggle to receive and trust in the forgiveness of God for acts he has committed in war for which he may have been objectively guilty. He may need help, not only in acknowledging his own unworthiness, but also in confessing and repenting of his offenses, and in receiving assurance of Christ's sufficient sacrifice for his sin.

In a high percentage of cases I've observed, especially among enlisted infantry, the soul conflict actually begins early, before exposure to combat, with a distressed childhood.It's often rooted in a childhood where parental moral guidance is lacking, inadequate, or in many cases even perverted.

This is not to ignore the truth that the ultimate root of all distress, conflict, and perversion is sin, the basic corruption of our human nature.

It's part of boys' natural growth and development to pit themselves against various kinds of opposing forces. And I observe that *boys who grow up without strong, true, and adequate moral guidance **consciously** pit themselves against moral boundaries, **deliberately** experiment with destructive behaviors*, and often ***ultimately** push aside moral restraints.* This is a familiar scenario among the many infantrymen I've personally known and worked with. It is as Proverbs 22:15 tells us: *"Foolishness is bound up in the heart of a child; the rod of discipline will remove it far from him."* But often the "rod of discipline" has been absent from these young men's lives. Or, in many cases it has been applied in perverse ways that drive out truth instead of foolishness.

What I've found sadly common is that they have been encouraged or even instructed in pushing aside moral

restraints, *by parents or other adult authority figures in their lives*. These persons have, for example, introduced them to pornography and trained them in drug use and criminality. An Army Intelligence agent told me that he left home running because his father was shooting at him! Another Army SGT recalled to me: *"My father's mental abuse caused me to go into combat with baggage that ripped my soul and spirit apart."*

I recall an event that took place at *The Anchor* servicemen's center in Oceanside, CA, when we were serving the Marines of Camp Pendleton. The event was humorous on the surface, but is a sad illustration of the "quality" of parental influence guiding many young infantry troops as they enter combat training and then war.

I was visiting with four Marines sitting at the counter of the center eating the lunch we had provided. As usual, I was chatting with the guys, moving from one to the other, getting to know their background, and introducing initial questions regarding their thoughts about God.

I left one of the men until last because he was talking on his cell phone. Although I never made an issue of the men's habits and language when they came into the center, yet out of respect they almost invariably scrubbed their language while they were in the place. Not so with the man on the phone! As I visited with the other guys, his language was smoking the air.

When he ended his call, as with the other men, I casually visited with him about his personal background, and then probed the question of his relationship with God. His response: "Oh, I'm saved." I kidded him with the words, "Well, your mouth isn't!"

He looked surprised and said, "Oh that on the phone? That was my mom. She's worse than I am!"

Where this is the case, then *the inner <u>conflict</u> begins at this early time* because, however distorted their upbringing may have been, *they have also lived in America,* and a high percentage of infantrymen come from the southern and southwestern parts of the country. There, *they have almost inevitably been touched and influenced by moral truth which, because it is truth, has unavoidably made its mark on their souls, as in the case of the "saved" young man just referred to.*

Studies, and simple observation, have shown that even the most prolific "killers" in combat, *struggle with the state of their soul.* An Army Special Operations chaplain friend says, *"...it will shut down any warrior if we tell him he is all right and he knows he is not all right."*

I've seen this often in young Marines, the majority of whom (literally, statistically) come from parts of the country where they have been immersed in church culture. They almost always have some acquaintance with Christianity and moral truth. Many, in fact, openly assert that they are "saved," even though their relationship to the Christian faith is confused, lacking true understanding, and conflicted.

A Special Forces MAJ friend adds:

"I echo the experience that many of the men do have a basic understanding/awareness of God from their lives prior to the Army. But they certainly do not necessarily have a right understanding of God and His grace, as many have had negative 'church' experiences in their past. This, of course, leaves them aware of a 'god,' but not necessarily a 'loving' and 'personal' Father."

So, as they approach the *role of killing* on behalf of their country, these young men commonly come with a **mixture of respect** and **bitterness** *toward God and biblical truth.* Where there is disrespect or resentment toward the version of religion they've known, it often leads them to *flaunt* their sinful freedoms. This in turn contributes to their enduring inner conflict when they have engaged in the act of killing and then begin to feel or consider the moral effects of it on their soul.

They know enough truth to sometimes begin to experience moral distress as they head into combat, but certainly enough to be morally fearful after they've been involved in mortal battle. There are also many who, because of their inability to face this moral conflict, consciously choose to fully abandon any moral restraints they've ever known, embracing the "trained killer" mentality, and repeating their perverse "translation" of Psalm 23: "Yea, though I walk through the valley of the shadow of death I will fear no evil, 'cause I'm the meanest….in the valley."

Although they may assure themselves that this moral abandonment has set them free from any moral accountability, of course they never escape their conscience and the truth they've heard. In their case I believe the soul conflict only goes farther "underground" as they consciously harden themselves. They may have abandoned any hope for themselves, but God and His truth have not abandoned them, and so we must not.

In a book I read recently, the author, a "black ops" intelligence operative, reveals his own example of the *abandonment of moral restraint, which is then challenged by conscience.* The author tells us that he has just finished an illicit sexual encounter with a female sergeant when she suddenly launches them into a discussion about death and heaven! They speculate about what heaven is like. Maybe it's whatever we believe it is; or maybe God will allow us to pick our heaven. Her ultimate conclusion is that heaven is, "feeling safe."

Since he has chosen to publish his moral abandonment on the pages of the book, he is compelled to attempt to make the conversation seem philosophical or spiritual. But, like it or not, **implanted in their souls** *is a belief in the reality of God, and a longing — especially now — for assurance that they can enjoy the benefits of being right with God, while their distorted and limited knowledge of Him and His Word leaves them conflicted and hopeless.*

The following comment by an Infantry MAJ friend (Ranger, combat Infantry leader in Iraq and Afghanistan) is a good example of a helpful, non-intrusive beginning in probing the warrior's spiritual conflict.

"The section on how the soul conflict begins in child-hood was very insightful for me. The idea that many of these young men grow up with very little parental guidance and yet a general sense of God and His justice (usually not His love). As I am a guy who always wants to get to the bottom line, my question is 'So, what do I do with this?' One thought is to encourage (caregivers) to get the guys to tell their stories of growing up — both good and bad. How did 'religion' play into their upbringing? These stories will provide insight into the way that they currently view God."

The combat veteran's unwillingness and/or inability to expose, face, and talk about his soul conflict is a complex thing, and it leaves him *feeling alone, as if looking through a glass wall at the "normal world." At this point many have become convinced that they can never again live on the other side of the glass.*

Again, my Special Forces MAJ friend says:

"There can be no expectations, and no judging. Each man is dealing with different 'baggage' from his past...and each has unique obstacles towards recovery. The timeline will be different for each man.

And the healing will absolutely be personal (which is why Jesus is ultimately the only true healer, as only He can be truly personal in each man's situation.). There is definitely a 'wall of protection' that each man puts up around himself as he goes through the experiences of war. This wall is built with different 'stones/ components' for each man, but it ultimately serves the same purpose for all: to create a buffer from being broken down, and rendered mission-incapable. As you identified, many build their walls with anger, bravado, and zeal. Most men choose to 'embrace' their duty to the point of letting it 'define them as men.' This often seems to happen because they have to choose between 'embracing their circumstances' or 'giving up'…and most men don't want to give up. This choice is often a 'survival mechanism choice,' however…and it ends up changing them as men, because they don't often get to truly 'let their hair down' and they have to push on…"

*Many of the psychological factors that influence the complexity and tenacity of this experience of chronic soul conflict are well known. **But in spiritual ministry we must look beneath the psychological symptoms** and discover the corresponding impact on the warrior's sense of his relationship with God.*

127

8.

PROMINENT FEATURES OF LONG-TERM SPIRITUAL HARM

B elow, I'll mention some of the familiar residual effects of combat operations, *along with their potentially lasting soul implications,* and then add some brief notes that I hope will provide some onramps to understanding and addressing the soul damage.

Bitterness *resulting from physical trauma* – "Why me?" Or, "Why my brother, and *not* me?" The warrior knows in his heart that this kind of "why" question is never answered in medical and psychological terms. The critical question is whether we as *spiritual caregivers* have *prepared ourselves* with the Word of Truth to address this fundamental question and guide the soul-damaged warrior to *the only One Who has the authority and transcendent perspective to **reply** to it.*

I say, "reply," rather than "answer," because the *beginning of peace* for the warrior is to learn what each of us caregivers surely understands, that the answer to *this kind* of "why" question is *unknowable to our time-bound minds.*

*It is as broad and deep and far-reaching as the **infinite wisdom** and **sovereign purposes** of God.* Peace and rest from this kind of lasting pain comes with learning that God's thoughts are far above our comprehension, and far more complex than can be laid out in a simple statement from finite perspective. The warrior *must be helped to take directly to God* the troubling thoughts of his own involvement in that which is brutal and unknowable, to find release from their grip.

Further, peace comes in learning to trust that God intends our good and will ultimately cause all things to work together to achieve good. This is the truth we and our soul-conflicted warrior friend must trust in, even though none of us has the perspective to see it all worked out from where we stand in this painful moment. We may not know how God can manage this sadness for the warrior's ultimate good, but He assures us in Jeremiah 29:11 that *He knows the plans He has, and they are for good, not for harm, to give our warrior friend a future and a hope.*

Perceived guilt, such as "survivor" guilt, or feelings borne of deadly or questionable acts he carried out under orders, or feeling that his failure has been the cause of someone else being killed or injured. *Perceived guilt may be rationally* *and legally analyzed and dismissed; but it is always related to deeper questions about the state of our soul before God.*

As ministers of God's Word, our unique value here is to help the warrior recognize that *his feelings at the moment are probably overpowering his rational thoughts*, and to help him address this question with humility and the assurance that flows out of the knowledge of ultimate truth.

His thoughts may sound like this: "Even if you assure me that I'm not objectively guilty of doing something wrong, I still have this persistent feeling that something is wrong with me, and I don't know how to fix the way I feel." As an example, with "survivor guilt," I've heard it put in words something like this: "I understand that I'm not wrong for being *here* at home, *but it still feels wrong that I'm not there with my unit. If I had been there, maybe my friend wouldn't have been killed."*

He needs our biblical perspective on guilt and God's sovereignty, our patient understanding, and sympathetic companionship; and these feelings will diminish over time.

Unresolved real guilt–The whole section on *forgiveness* further down is critical to this issue. Real guilt cannot be resolved when the warrior *doesn't dare open his heart to anyone else because of fear and shame*, and doesn't have the depth of relationship with God that allows him to go directly to Him for forgiveness and cleansing.

Yet in his heart he knows that only God has the authority to *resolve guilt*, which is to *forgive sin*. In this, even the caregiver's wisdom and compassion only become adequate when he or she has formed a relationship of trust with the warrior, and has been welcomed to guide him into the biblical assurances spoken of in the section on forgiveness.

Pain of bringing to mind brutal memories or images – This can be one of the most devastating and remorseless features of emotional and spiritual damage to the warrior. Behavioral and cognitive counseling therapies can help to diminish the intensity, and frequency of such memories, but the "body" long remembers what the conscious mind fervently desires to forget. The *hurt* *the soul feels from such memories is really impossible to describe.*

Going beneath the emotions, into the deeper questions of the *spirit* will wield the most power in healing both emotions and soul.

It may help, for example, to consider the question, "What *makes these memories and images 'brutal'? Why does it* *trouble us at all to see a person blow himself and others* *into oblivion, or to see a child whose eyes have been gouged* *out and then he's been used as a sex slave in the name and* *authority of Christless religion?"*

It is certainly *not merely* because we haven't seen these things before. It's not just because they're new and surprising to us, for then we'd react like an animal...we'd flinch and walk on. Or else we'd quickly adapt to this new reality, accept it and move on. I'm not being facetious. When we see the ocean or the mountains for the first time we're not left with dreadful memories we would call "brutal."

The events that create these images are expressions of *broken human nature that will one day fall under the righteous judgment of God.* This opens the way for the warrior to see these things in relationship to the One Who will ultimately bring righteous judgment; and Who longs to bring each one of us *to a place of rest in His ultimate judgment* of human behavior.

This place of rest is not that the warrior is set free *from true grieving,* but from his furious, frustrated, helpless, overpowering feeling of *personal responsibility to punish and end this evil,* which I believe is one of the hidden powers behind the nightmares and re-experiencing of the events.

However, since I know that my own brother, like many other true believers and followers of Christ, is *still brutalized* by re-experiencing such dreadful memories and images after more than forty years since Vietnam, I acknowledge that there can be such a deep etching of ruthless images like these on the soul that they may never in this life be fully erased... only managed and controlled by the Spirit of God through persevering prayer and longsuffering support of those close and dear to the warrior.

Fear of further harm – This refers to both the warrior's professional career safety, and other people's personal judgment of him. In either case, he knows that he can be hurt further by exposing his distressed thoughts and feelings. The soul-damaged warrior is left with the *feeling* that there really isn't *anyone* he can trust with the deepest fears and aching thoughts of his heart. In his sense of danger *he feels safer talking to no one.*

He needs to know that there is *One Who already knows his deepest thoughts, loves him perfectly, judges righteously, and can forgive and protect him ultimately, regardless of human perceptions and outcomes.*

He will need a friend who has been found trustworthy, to help him *take hold of* this soul-freeing truth about God. If he is a believer, he needs support in rediscovering the truth about God's merciful, gracious and sovereign nature. If he does not yet believe, he needs help to understand *how* and *why* to turn in trust to the only One who can cleanse his soul and grant him the *spiritual safety* he needs to face the *temporal dangers* his soul fears.

Wariness of support efforts – Dr. Croft and Chaplain Parker give a lot of insights about this in their book. They tell of the warriors' rejection of "clipboard PTSD assessments," and the difficulty for the warrior of *even processing* such instruments, considering the impact war has had on their cognitive skills. They point out, as I have also done above, the fear trauma-tized warriors have of experiencing further damage to their military careers through the exposure of their "problems," even though it is in theory forbidden to penalize combatants for acknowledging symptoms of PTSD. The authors assure us that, where "clipboard assessments" may create wariness, the investment of time in *more personalized*, human care are appreciated and effective in treatment of PTSD.

A Special Operations chaplain friend confirms that: *"Patient love that sticks it out is what is required. They need fathers and brothers..."*

The point here is the warrior's *respect and trust for the caregiver.* As spiritual caregivers, if by our love, patience, and understanding we can earn their respect, then doors into their heart will be opened.

Dread of negative peer reactions – Whether he faces the question consciously or merely "senses" it; whether it is spoken or unspoken by his peers; when the warrior begins to realize his need for help, he *will* face the question: "How will I be treated by my 'brothers' if I don't continue with them in their memory-and-emotion-deadening activities, but rather pursue actual recovery?"

We can provide him some assurance regarding this question. From personal experience, I know that when a warrior responds to help *that is offered in the Name of Christ*, his brothers will *usually be sympathetic* to his relationship with us, and not antagonistic. He is no longer a new "boot," who is to be hazed and indoctrinated by peers and seniors; but rather a "brother," who has shared their experience in combat. This sympathy may be out of respect for a "brother," or out of their personal respect for the Lord, or even out of a hidden longing on their own behalf. In any case, we may reassure him of the probable support of his peers if he turns to us for help in the Name of Christ.

Fear of "exposure" before those whose opinions are most precious to them–That is, *"If I expose my 'filthiness' will I irreparably destroy the image some very important person or persons have of me?"*

After sharing with me some serious struggles he was having, a Special Operations SGT friend told me that it "tears at my soul almost every day, and it's hard to tell my wife or family."

We may be the stepping-stones our warrior friend needs toward taking the risk of opening himself to others. As servants of God, no one has a higher regard for appropriate confidentiality than you and I, because we know *ourselves* to be sinners, redeemed solely by the mercy and grace of God. We understand the depths of sin possible in our own human nature, the fear of exposure, and the depths of God's love and forgiveness. As the warrior tests us and finds us faithful, he may begin to open himself to others. With this perspective, we are in a position to guide him through his fear of the loss of the respect of those dear to him.

However tenacious the chronic spiritual harm and soul conflict produced in the warrior by engaging in combat, the scripture-guided caregiver can help set his fearful soul free from:

- *The conviction that he has no right to be helped,*
- *The conviction that he deserves to suffer endless temporal condemnation, and*
- *His hopelessness about talking with anyone.*

9.

SPECIAL SECTION

HELPFUL READING

I've already mentioned several valuable books, and have tried hard to adequately articulate some of the lessons I've learned from the authors' experience and gifted communication. Through the skill of these writers, I've been taught so much about the world of our men and women at war, and my understanding of how to reach out to them has been so transformed, that I have to ask your forgiveness in advance for being so direct in what I'll say next.

If we are seriously interested in helping post-deployment warriors recover from their emotional and spiritual trauma, then unless we've been there personally, **how can we not be reading the best materials written for our understanding of the world they operate in?**

To desire to minister to them meaningfully and effectively without becoming as familiar with their operational world as possible would be like a person trying to perform surgery without studying anatomy and physiology, or a police officer trying to effectively serve his community without knowing its streets and neighborhoods.

Did I overwork that point? I pray God will deliver us from imagining that we can minister to soul-damaged warriors out of the assumption that there is anything comparable in our local experience to the world of war that has absorbed them and transformed them.

To assist you if you decide to take advantage of the valuable reading resources that are available, below are two lists of books I've read and been helped by. *For your help and convenience I'm recommending some, cautioning about some, and strongly urging that some be read.*

I'll also note some websites. But be thoughtful, as websites contain lots of collateral information and links that *may not be as useful or reliable as the home site and main presenter.* Some will contain links to secular materials contrary to our Christian perspective, or Christian sites that are doctrinally shallow or questionable.

There is a bibliography at the back of the book; but knowing how bibliographies are usually used...that is to say, not used, unless the reader is doing research...I'm placing this list here in the heart of the book, hoping it will stir you to take advantage of these important resources.

Many of the books I'm reading are written by caregivers, *about the warriors and their families*, regarding the impact of combat operations, and approaches to healing and restoration.

I've also selected books that allow me as much as possible to *taste* their real life in combat. It helps a bit that I have personally felt their fear and other emotions, having been in Vietnam with my wife and baby during the Tet Offensive in 1968. I believe the most meaningful way to get a taste of the world today's warrior lives in — apart from personal conversations with the warriors — is to **read the writings by the warriors themselves,** *or at least those of deeply embedded and sympathetic journalists.*

SUPPORT BOOKS AND STUDIES

This first list of books consists of those written by or about the warriors *with the goal of support and recovery*.

Nam Vet, Making Peace With Your Past – Dean-Cantrell – WordSmith.

Chuck Dean served as an Airborne soldier in Vietnam, and Bridget Cantrell is a psychologist with the experience and heart to care for warriors.

Once A Warrior, Wired For Life – Dean-Cantrell – Hearts Toward Home Int'l

When The War Is Over A New One Begins – Dean-Nordberg – Contact: Point Man Ministries.

Down Range To Iraq And Back – Dean-Cantrell – Hearts Toward Home Int'l

Souls Under Siege, The Effects of Multiple Troop Deployments – and **How to Weather the Storm.** Cantrell–Hearts Toward Home Int'l

Heroes At Home – Kay – Bethany House

War Zone, Hope Beyond Carnage – Brown – CSNBooks

The Combat Trauma Healing Manual – Adsit – Military Ministry Press–Campus Crusade/Cru

Hope Unseen – Smiley – Howard Books/Simon & Schuster

Souls In Transition, The Religious & Spiritual Lives Of Emerging Adults – Christian Smith with Patricia Snell – Oxford University Press

This is a statistical study, textbook-style, by two University of Notre Dame professors. It analyzes the changing religious and spiritual attitudes and experiences of "emerging adults," specifically those between the ages of seventeen and twenty-three. It is interesting and useful in understanding the pool of young people from which our modern military is drawn.

Website – Article by Ltc (Ret.) David Grossman – Dave provided a link in his letter to me, but did not provide a website address that I could copy and paste in here. For your use I found the following website that featured his article. The website looks interesting, but I'm not a member and do not intend this as a referral. This is specifically for your access to Dave's article. http://www.recoverytoday. net/2011/55-august/350-the-myth-of-our-returning-veterans-and-violent-crime

Website – heartstowardhome.com – for the works of Chuck Dean and Dr. Bridget Cantrell.

Website – combatfaith.com – Recommended by my friend, an Army Infantry MAJ, for materials by and about Allen Clarke, writer/speaker, double amputee from Vietnam. Sort out the best of his works, and links on his website.

Soldiers No More–Reader's Digest Article – June 2012

This is a good article about the difficulty and discouragement combatants face in attempting to return to civilian life and the potentially frustrating job search.

I Always Sit With My Back To The Wall – Dr. Harry A. Croft, M.D., with Rev. Dr. Chrys Parker, J.D. – Stillpoint Media Services.

This book is a collaboration between a male research psychiatrist and a female therapist with background in law, religion, and counseling. *Psychologically, it is one of the most compassionate, practical, and balanced that I've read.* It is written *to the warrior with PTSD*, and is focused on practical help, while also acknowledging the frustrating mixed messages the warrior may have been receiving between the medical and psychological communities. I strongly recommend it for those reasons.

***Website* – Article: "Will God Forgive?"** – Nathan Martin–
OMF.org>US>Peoples and Places>Stories>Cambodia
Stories> Will God Forgive?

This is an unusual and moving article *on forgiveness for the warrior,* from the experience of a newly believing soldier in Cambodia who had served in Pol Pot's harsh Khmer Rouge regime, and now struggled with the memory of killing, and the question of forgiveness.

Faith In The Fog Of War–vol. II – Christopher Plekenpol–
In-Him Ministries

This volume is a devotional, based on the original book. Each chapter consists of devotional thoughts developed out of Plekenpol's war experiences as a combat officer.

Building The Warrior Brain – Reader's Digest
Article – Kathryn Wallace – February 2013

BOOKS ON THE *EXPERIENCE* OF WAR

The following reading is about the **experience** of war. I urge you not to consider this merely optional or "extra curricular" reading. As I have said, it is the way of "tasting" the warrior's real life in combat.

Herein is the *true* study of the *person at war*. Nothing has helped me more in this ministry than "seeing and hearing" him in the midst of the experience. No explanations or stories *about* him match this kind of exposure. Again, it's the reason for including the list in the heart of this book. If you are one who desires to minister to the soul of the warrior, please select at least some of these books and read them. Some are written by believers, and are especially instructive and inspirational.

Several of these books are from an Army Times recommended reading list; some are on the Marine Corps Commandant's recommended reading list; and others have been recommended to me by men "in the fight."

As you seek to understand and minister to warriors, these books will help you taste their excitement, fear, hyper-vigilant tension, discomfort, dark humor, elation, anxiety, anger, loyalty, self-sacrifice, selfishness, brotherly bonds, hatreds, spiritual hope/doubt/conflict, toughness, weakness, hypocrisies, attitudes toward politicians and leadership, and lots more...all super-intensified by the ugly self-contradictions of war.

I don't recommend *all* the books on the list to *everyone*. In some, the language and imagery are extremely strong and may be shocking and overly offensive. But if you are dealing with combatants, and you want to gain understanding of their hearts and be less of a "stranger" to their suffering, then please consider reading some of them.

Your Base, Post, or local library will have many of them, and they're easy to find by title on Amazon.

On Killing, The Psychological Cost of Learning To Kill in War and Society – Grossman – Back Bay Books

I believe this book is foundational to understanding the preparation of a warrior and the impact of war.

The Faith of The American Soldier – Mansfield – Charisma House

Masters of Chaos, The Secret History of The Special Forces – Robinson – PublicAffairs

From Basic To Baghdad, A Soldier Writes Home – Hogan – Brave Ideas

Kill Bin Laden – Fury – St. Martin's Griffin

Generation Kill – Wright – Berkley Caliber

Moment of Truth In Iraq – Yon – RVB

The Unforgiving Minute, A Soldier's Education – Mullaney – The Penguin Press

Not A Good Day To Die, The Untold Story of Operation Anaconda – Naylor – Berkley Caliber

American Heroes, In The Fight Against Radical Islam – North – B&H Books

The Blog Of War, Front-Line Dispatches From Soldiers In Iraq – Burden – Simon & Schuster

Forever A Soldier, Unforgettable Stories of Wartime Service – Wiener – Nat. Geographic

Whiskey Tango Foxtrot, A Photographer's Chronicle of The Iraq War – Gilbertson – Chicago

Ghost Wars, The Secret History of The CIA, Afghanistan and Bin Laden from the Soviet Invasion to September 10, 2001 – Coll – Penguin Books

The Taliban and The Crisis of Afghanistan – Crews, Tarzi – Harvard Univ. Press

House To House, An Epic Memoir of War – Bellavia – Simon & Schuster

Descent Into Chaos: The U.S. and the Disaster in Pakistan, Afghanistan, and Central Asia – Rashid – Penguin Press

Ambush Alley: The Most Extraordinary Battle Of The Iraq War – Pritchard – Presidio Press

The Forever War – Filkins – Alfred A. Knopf, New York

All Quiet On The Western Front – Remarque – Ballantine Books – New York

The Only Thing Worth Dying For – Eric Blehm – Harper

Hope Unseen – Smiley – Howard Books/Simon & Schuster.

The author, Scotty Smiley is a believer, and this is one of the most touching and inspirational books I've read. Please read it.

War – Junger – Hatchette Book Group

The author is one of the most powerfully articulate war correspondents I've read. I wish I could quote half his book for you...or better still, I hope that you will read it.

American Heroes In Special Operations – North – Fidelis Books

Victory Point – Ed Darack – Berkley Caliber Books

A Nightmare's Prayer – Michael Franzak – Threshold Editions/Simon & Schuster

As You Were: To War and Back With the Black Hawk Battalion of the Virginia National Guard – Davenport – John Wiley & Sons

Blood Brothers – Weisskopf – Henry Holt and Company

None Left Behind, The 10th Mountain Division and The Triangle Of Death – Sasser – St. Martins Press

Operation Dark Heart – Shaffer – St. Martins Press

The 188th Crybaby Brigade – Joel Chasnoff – Free Press

A Privilege To Die, Inside Hezbollah's Legions and Their Endless War Against Israel – Thanassis Cambanis – Free Press

Kill or Capture, How a Special Operations Task Force Took Down A Notorious Al Qaeda Terrorist – Matthew Alexander – St. Martin's

Inside the Revolution: How the Followers of Jihad, Jefferson & Jesus Are Battling to Dominate the Middle East and Transform The World – Joel C. Rosenberg – Tyndale

The Wrong War – Bing West – Random House

Afghanistan, Graveyard of Empires. A New History of the Borderland – David Isby – Pegasus Books

Endless War – Ralph Peters – Stackpole Books

The Strong Horse, Power, Politics, and The Clash Of Arab Civilizations – Lee Smith – Doubleday

This book, like the one preceding it on the list, is not actually an account of our troops' experience of war. Both books are rather an analysis of the context of the "asymmetric" war they are called to fight. These two books are about the "schizophrenic" world — Lee Smith's word — of the Arabs, from millennia past, and the influence of Islam, introduced 600 years after Jesus' earthly ministry.

Shadow of the Sword, A Marine's Journey of War, Heroism, and Redemption – Jeremiah Workman with John R. Bruning – Presidio Press of Random House

Hunters, U.S. Snipers In The War On Terror—Milo S. Afong—Penguin Group, (USA) Inc.

They Fought For Each Other—Kelly Kennedy—St. Martin's.

This book, written by a female Army Times reporter who was embedded with a company of the 26th infantry regiment out of Schweinfurt, Germany, is one of the best, saddest, and strongest I've read on the Iraq war. I highly recommend it.

Outlaw Platoon—Sean Parnell, with John Bruning—William Morrow/HarperCollins Publishers

This book about a platoon of the 10th Mtn. Div. in Afghanistan eloquently and emotionally takes one into the life, feelings, and heart of good troops in hard combat. It is also one of those replete with the strongest language.

Lions of Kandahar—Major Rusty Bradley and Kevin Maurer—Bantam Books/Random House

No Way Out—Mitch Weiss and Kevin Maurer—Berkley

What It Is Like To Go To War—Karl Marlantes—Atlantic Monthly Press.

This book has some strong, informative elements, some of which I'll refer to as I write further. But Marlantes summarizes his spiritual perspective by propounding a mixture of mythology and psychology as a means of addressing the physical, emotional, and "spiritual" issues of the warrior.

Fearless – Eric Blehm – WaterBrook Press.

This is a book that I recommend from my heart. The story of believing SEAL TEAM SIX Operator, Adam Brown, is powerfully inspiring. Please read it.

Sua Ponte, The Forging Of A Modern American Ranger – Dick Couch – Berkley Books

No Easy Day, The Autobiography Of A Navy SEAL – Mark Owen with Kevin Maurer – Penguin Group (USA)

SEAL TEAM SIX, Memoirs Of An Elite Navy SEAL Sniper – Howard E. Wasdin and Stephen Templin – St. Martins Press

I especially recommend this book *as a means of gaining insight into the super strong, honor-motivated, ego-influenced, spiritually complex heart of the "First Tier" Special Operations warrior.* In the course of the book the author reveals faint occasional references to his spiritual thoughts...mingled with slightly restrained strong language. In his acknowledgements at the close of the book, he refers directly to his personal faith in the Lord Jesus Christ.

TWO WARS – Nate Self – Tyndale House

This is another book I truly recommend. As a Ranger Platoon Leader, Silver Star and Purple Heart winner, Nate Self takes us with him into one of the most vicious, prolonged, high-altitude firefights in the war on terror. And then he allows us into the sad and frightening war within his soul during several years following combat. He is a true believer who spends a chapter of his book sharing the wrenching struggle he went through *during combat*, when one of his young Rangers *thought* he heard him utter the Lord Jesus Christ's name in vain during a firefight. The book is wonderfully summed up in an "*Afterword*" written by Stu Weber, pastor, former Green Beret, and author of *Tender Warrior*.

The Red Circle, My Life In The Navy SEAL Sniper Corps And How I Trained America's Deadliest Marksmen – Brandon Webb – St. Martin's Press

SEAL TARGET GERONIMO – Chuck Pfarrer – St. Martin's Press

This is an "insider's" account of the killing of Osama bin Laden. It is a bit more historical and scholarly book than some of the others, and the use of vulgar language is restrained.

Battle Ready, Memoir of a SEAL Warrior Medic – Mark L. Donald – St. Martin's Press

The author, both a warrior and a combat medic, is recipient of the nation's second highest award for valor. He speaks of his faith in God, even as he describes the war trauma that nearly took it from him. This is his sincere personal description of his patriotism, relationships, war experiences, love of serving warriors medically, and his own battle with PTSD. His story is like taking an intense course in what it means to serve self-sacrificially, and to suffer greatly as the price of service. If you read this book you will *know* the *soul-damaged warrior* like never before.

10.

WHERE DOES A WARRIOR TURN FOR STRENGTH AND GUIDANCE?

In the battle — when a warrior is feeling stressed, afraid, confused, trapped — he doesn't usually turn to the Lord's Word and meditate on God's Wisdom. He's in survival mode, muscle memory, autopilot. He may try to pray, but usually briefly and without conscious expectancy.

He needs help *now — in advance of the fight*, between deployments, following the battle, *any time* he will allow us into his heart — to *find and know God* through His Word; and in finding God, to find wisdom and understanding that are truly relevant to his unique needs as a combatant...*the knowledge of God **that will permeate his mind** in the midst of the consuming chaos of battle.*

Practical examples soldiers share of help they *did **not*** receive in combat situations *can be instructive in the kind of preparation we ourselves need,* to help them prepare.

In his powerful book, *War*, Sebastian Junger provides a simple, direct example of this. He relates a moment when a soldier decided to tell him about a conversation with his battalion chaplain. The soldier relates to the chaplain his own limited understanding of the gospel...that, basically, God came down to earth in the form of Christ and died for our sins, to which the chaplain agreed. And then that Jesus died a painful death, *knowing* He was going to heaven. Again the chaplain agreed. Then the soldier revealed the question that was disturbing him. *How is Jesus' sacrifice greater than that of a soldier in this valley who has no idea whether he's going to heaven?*

Our hearts ache for the soldier, as he reports that he received "no useful response." But this turns the question back to us, **how would we** — ministers of the trustworthy and understandable Word of God — respond to the SGT's *sincere but misguided question* in a way that would set him on a path of *truth*, *meaning*, and *hope* as he stepped back into the line of fire? Or, if I know him prior to his deployment, how would I prepare him to answer such a question for himself, when he enters the valley of personal sacrifice?

In his book, *What It Is Like To Go To War*, Marine Platoon Leader Karl Marlantes finds himself seething inside following a visit by a chaplain who flew in to their besieged jungle site at great personal risk...bringing the men "Southern Comfort" and a fresh batch of dirty jokes.

He asked himself how he could be angry at a guy who had risked his life to cheer him up. Then, even though he does not present himself in the book as a Christian believer, he realized that in a situation "approaching the sacred in its terror and contact with the infinite," he needed a *spiritual guide*, not liquor and dirty jokes.

Don't misunderstand my point. I know from personal experience in Vietnam and other countries of S.E. Asia during that conflict that the vast majority of chaplains in the military were faithful believers who had "run to the spiritual fight" while "ministerial" hirelings fled to safe places. I'm confident that Marlantes had contact with godly chaplains during his combat experience, and that he selected this particular event to make his point about the *need for spiritual guidance,* and in fact *his point is true.*

The event he chose and his application of it further high-light the question for us: *what are we providing* our warrior friends in anticipation of those times that "approach the sacred in terror and contact with the infinite"?

Are *we* ready, first in advance of combat, and then after the damage has been done, to help them sort through their fears, misunderstandings, guilt, and questions, with gracious, supportive guidance? Can we help them *find God Himself,* and trust in *His sovereign oversight of life and death in the context of war?*

Proverbs 14:10, 13 – *"The heart knows its own bitterness, and a stranger does not share its joy....even in laughter the heart may be in pain, and the end of joy may be grief."*

That verse refers to a major reason for silence among PTS and COS sufferers. And it's also a reason they find it hard to respond to the support of "strangers"—even well-meaning counselors and family members who are "strangers" to their suffering.

Proverbs 25:20 adds a barb to the point—*"Like one who takes off a garment on a cold day, or like vinegar on soda, is he who sings songs to a troubled heart."*

We can see a touching example of this well-meaning insensitivity in Scotty Smiley's book, *Hope Unseen.*

He admits that, although he had read the Bible and believed it, now lying in a hospital bed he was not sure what he believed. *How can a blinded warrior understand a loving God?* He felt betrayed. And the "sappy symphony" of friends swirling around him in his hospital room praying, singing praise songs and laughing made him "want to puke."

If we desire to help them we need to learn how *not* to be "strangers," how *not* to increase their pain by our "songs." It can be done through the humble preparatory labor of learning, listening, and gracious probing.

Proverbs 20:5 – *"A plan in the heart of a man is like deep water, but a man of understanding draws it out."*

This verse affirms that however deep the matter may be in the heart, a *true friend with true understanding* — not thoughtless off-the-shelf Bible references or shelf-stock psychological knowledge — *can draw it out.*

Chaplain Mike Hoyt adds the following comments:

"...most importantly, the scriptural answers must flow from a variety of contexts simultaneously, and that is the challenge and the interpretive wisdom needed. Consider this: the first context is that of the counselor him/herself; the second is the soul condition of the (war-traumatized) counselee; the third is the context of the truth of the scripture in its place as it appears in the biblical record; the fourth is the (blending) of all these competing contexts into some usable form for all concerned.

"This is less about providing answers and more about fashioning a life strategy that reintegrates personhood in relationship to a forgiving and empowering God... We don't use scripture to 'fix' us or others. Scripture reads us, tells us what God thinks of us and our human dilemma. It reveals His nature and redemptive plan while it lays bare our condition and need for His redemption. "

Consider:

Proverbs 14:30, 15:13, and 17:22 – *"A tranquil heart is life to the body..." "A joyful heart makes a cheerful face, but when the heart is sad the spirit is broken." "...a broken spirit dries up the bones."*

Proverbs 25:28 — *"Like a city that is broken into and without walls is a man who has no control over his spirit."*

Proverbs 18:14 reminds us of what every warrior knows – that if a man's spirit is strong he can bear up under incredible physical sickness or wounds. *"But as for a broken spirit who can bear it?"* This man feels helpless, hopeless, without any strength to fight the war that rages *within*.

The verses above are a *soul* description of PTSD.

Doctor Harry Croft, in *I Always Sit With My Back To The Wall*, articulates a compassionate natural perspective. Seeking to understand the whole person, he says that much of Western medicine tends to view the body as a machine that may be "fixed" with drugs, and procedures. But he believes that a human being is far more complex and integrated than this. In keeping with this, he believes that PTSD is in a unique class of disorders because it is psychological and neurobiological at the same time.

This is a helpful medical perspective of that condition described in Proverbs by Solomon. It's also a reason why PTSD can be such a confusing, devastating, and tenacious condition.

Dr. Croft credits "Nature" for this wonderfully complex interworking of body and mind, and whatever it is that is "greater than the sum of their parts." Because it is "natural," even this wise medical insight leaves open the issue of *soul damage…spiritual hopelessness and sense of separation from God*.

Examples abound of men in combat oblivious to their own serious physical wounds helping injured comrades, while — as in one example I'm thinking of — another man may be sitting against a wall staring at nothing. Corresponding to this, suicides are tragically familiar occurrences among combatants. When the spirit is unbearably broken, the inner response of the warrior may sound something like this: "If I kill my body, I kill the *consciousness* of this *pain in my soul.*" *This is a foundational expression of hopelessness.*

The warrior who finds himself to be *"Like a city that is broken into and without walls…who has no control (or has lost control) over his spirit"* has one great, immanent need. It is *__hope__*…not just temporal, momentary hope that he'll make it home alive from this dreadful deployment, but *hope in God…* hope that genuinely reaches beyond death.

He needs the hope that is rooted in true understanding of God; hope that shepherds him out of the devastation war has done to his spirit, and guides him through the fear of the further challenges he knows he'll face as he tries to reintegrate into the world of "the normals."

*The question is **how to help him find hope?*** Discovering the answer, as always, will be subject to our willingness to *first listen with our heart until we know the unique individual that our warrior is, and the root of the trauma he's experiencing.* Some elements of this will be common to any warrior. But again, what each individual "brought with him" to war must influence our understanding, and will certainly influence how we may minister to him without being dismissed as "strangers" whose words fall on benumbed ears.

I recently read some news articles and heard the testimony of an Army psychologist who went to war in Iraq with his soldiers and poured his heart into helping them — as he described it — "make it one more day." After he left active service and returned to teaching, the destruction war had wrought in his own spirit overwhelmed him and, at age forty-two, without hope, he ended his own life. As I read and listened to this tragic account, it was apparent that he went to war with energy and devotion to the soldiers, *but with no personal grasp of ultimate truth that transcended war.* He battled on behalf of his soldiers and himself with education and dedication, but out of a spiritual void that left him unable to find hope for himself beyond the carnage.

Here are some questions to ask *ourselves* as we listen for the heart of our warrior friend and seek to help him find God's path to new hope:

First, *Is he spiritually lost?* He may be one who has no grasp of ultimate truth that transcends war, who has realized the insanity of daily laying his life down in front of the machines of war without any ultimate *meaning* to whether he lives or dies. He may not understand the war he's fighting, but he must be helped to understand the ultimate meaning of death and life and eternity.

Is he a believer whose spirit is twisted around the question of killing other human beings...some of whom *his* bullets may have consigned to eternal separation from God? This is a far more confusing and complex issue for some of our warriors than we may have realized, especially in the "asymmetrical" war they're fighting. This is *not* the "simple" question, "Is it right to kill in war?" Killing is *real* and *personal* to them. Some are saying in their hearts, "I didn't just 'kill someone in war'; I killed a human being who undoubtedly does not know the only Mediator between God and man. And now he will *never* have that opportunity."

My Special Operations chaplain friend, who is himself a decorated warrior, helps us understand the seriousness of this issue in these words:

"Part of the problem is that we speak in terms of 'just war,' and not (in terms of) **killing**. *Who really gives a rip about Augustine's just war theory? It is guidelines for nations to go to war not for people killing others. A large part of the criteria for modern just war theory is based around facts and intelligence that we will never know (or at least not for a number of years).*

"Warriors, as you have pointed out, continually struggle with the question of whether they are okay. Oftentimes men going assuming the mantle of warrior have not even thought about this issue. Their entire concept of warfare is based on their choice of books and movies. Some are raised on movies such as The Longest Day *and other simple heroic struggles of good vs. evil. Others may be focused on the post-modern*

notion of the troubled hero who experiences the hell of war yet displays super human ability to rise above it and even to be unaffected in the long run.

"Warriors need to understand the morality of killing prior to being engaged in it. We give them rules of engagement written by lawyers to ensure that we follow the law of war. It deals with the minimum standard rather than the highest standard. Few are willing to explore the morality of killing and help prepare our warriors for what they will face. We help them with the technical details of shooting and tactics but do not prepare them for the reality of killing.

"In the aftermath of the horror of war, warriors look for approval of what they have done. They look first to their comrades. If the men around them do not approve either of them or their conduct then most everything else is meaningless. As you mentioned, sometimes this emerges as the desire to recreate the closeness and camaraderie they previously experienced. Often this is combined with dangerous or harmful activities.

"They also look for approval from their leaders. We award medals for a very good reason–it is a source of encouragement for that person and to encourage similar behavior. Most warriors when awarded valor

awards do not accept that it was them, but rather the team that accomplished something. Yet most acknowledge and fight hard to award these same medals to their own soldiers. This can cause serious conflict when these awards are given to those who have done wrong or believe they have done wrong.

"Even if our warriors are confident in the justice of their cause, are prepared as well as possible for the reality of killing, and well grounded in all areas of their relationship with God, they must struggle with the same conflict illustrated by medieval writers. We may be objectively innocent of guilt in the taking of other lives, (and yet) we still have the problem of our sinful heart. Is it possible to be blameless in the death of our enemies and yet be in sin because we harbor anger and bitterness in our heart? No one is exempt from the sins of our heart even when we are innocent of what most would consider the obvious sin."

In his book, *Fearless*, about the life of Adam Brown, a believing SEAL TEAM SIX member, author Eric Blehm reports that Adam struggled with this very spiritual pain.

During an operation at Easter time, Adam was walking slumped as though he were ill. When he was asked if he was okay, Adam told his teammate that he was troubled because he had killed men — sent them to hell — on the morning of his Savior's resurrection.

Is he a person — believer or unbeliever — whose spirit is so sick of killing, so worn out by not knowing whether he'll be alive or dead tomorrow that he can't go on? Solomon asks, "as for a broken spirit, who can bear it?" Our part is to recognize the brokenness and — before brokenness becomes utter despair — to *wisely discern the nature of the brokenness and lead the warrior to transcendent hope.*

God promises through the Apostle Paul in **Romans 8:11** that, *"...if the Spirit of Him who raised Jesus from the dead dwells in you, He who raised Christ Jesus from the dead will also give life ('animate, arouse and invigorate, restore life') to your mortal bodies through His Spirit Who dwells in you."*

John 14:26-27; Romans 5:1; Philippians 4:6-7; Colossians 1:19-22 – all remind us that there is a peace that can be imparted to the war-troubled soul by God Himself, that is *other* than — that *transcends* — normal human psychology or comprehension.

A fellow Cadence missionary, whom I quoted earlier about war-induced anger, says there were three steps that he experienced in being set free from the raging anger that had taken up residence in his life.

First, he had to recognize and acknowledge to himself what was happening...that he was still bound up by the power of his residual anger, and that it was being expressed destructively toward others, including those most dear to him.

Second, he had to confess it to others (first his wife) who were affected by it. In his case the brokenness and confession took place in a church service.

Third, those who heard his confession gathered around him and prayed God would set him free from it. It was at this time that he felt the deep anger taken away, and replaced by peace.

This was not a mere "myth ritual," but a *peace* that had been *imparted by God*.

Here is an important summary of the passages referred to above:

The restoration of peace and joy to the _heart_ initiates the restoration of the _outer_ man, and ultimately makes _relational_ healing possible.

For the warrior, deep and lasting healing begins with being helped to gain *true knowledge of where he stands, not only on the emotional/psychological spectrum, but before the God Who loves him limitlessly and is able to restore his soul, body, and relational being.*

From this point he may be helped to understand the depths of God's grace and mercy...and also forgiveness where that may be needed. We may then go on to help him translate: *forgiveness* to *hope*, to *thankfulness*, to *joy*, to the *re-awakening of the outer man*, to the *restoration of relational strength*.

11.

WHAT DO I SAY TO A
SOUL-DAMAGED WARRIOR?

*Proverbs 18:2, 13 – "A fool does not delight in
understanding, but only in revealing his own mind...
He who gives an answer before he hears, it is folly
and shame to him."*

If a warrior turns to us for help in dealing with the effects
of combat operations, we're forcefully reminded by these
proverbs that *listening, praying*, and *searching the scriptures*
are our *most important work*.

When we want to help we usually try too hard. We think
we need to figure out what we're supposed to say, and then
start talking. We usually do this without any sense of "where
the person is" that we're trying to help. Before trying to say
something helpful, we've got to learn to listen. We need *not*
try hard to *answer* correctly, but try hard to *hear more deeply*

and accurately. "Like apples of gold in settings of silver is a word spoken in right circumstances." Proverbs 25:11

If we hear well, our initial response may be tears and profound silence. Talking to one who is suffering, feeling his pain, longing to be able to take away the pain and set him free…this is a difficult and emotional ministry. And it is *not* intended as a brief cathartic experience for the caregiver. To relieve our own stress after a conversation with a soul-damaged warrior by simply breathing a sigh of relief and putting the hurtful thoughts behind us until the next conversation *would be to forfeit some of the most important work of this ministry.*

I urge that, whether or not we have counseling training, we embrace the tremendously important follow-up work of *making notes* **_after_** *our conversations…reflecting, thinking deeply and seriously.*

While reflecting and praying for the warrior after conversing with him, *God reveals much more to me* as I ask myself, and ask God:

1. *What have I actually heard?* This discipline helps me get beyond hearing what I was expecting to hear, or wanting to hear.
2. *What did I not hear?* What *seemed to go unsaid* that stirred my heart and made me long to know him more deeply and lift the unspoken pain from his spirit?
3. *What did I miss during the conversation that, on reflection, I now realize?* Sometimes I will recall a

vocal inflection, a reaction, a flash of anger, a limited confession, a hint of fear, a silence…any newly realized awareness that may grant a deeper or further understanding of the war that's still being fought in my friend's soul.

4. How can I better express my compassion and support in our next conversation?

I have a believing friend in U. S. Embassy security in Afghanistan. Moved by some extremely evil events he has witnessed in the area, he poured out his heartfelt, "Where is God?" questions in an email message.

I wrote back right away to see how he is handling the questions, and whether he wants to talk about it. He replied that he was *not* finding answers and *does* want to talk. So far so good…but as I prepared to do the scriptural research and help him find answers, *suddenly the Lord reminded me that I had hardly acknowledged the angry frustration and impotence he was feeling that caused this outburst. If I immediately launched into providing theological answers I would have initially missed the main point for him, which was his impotent rage at the wickedness he was witnessing.*

This brought me back to the question, "How can I better express my compassion and support?" I hope I'll be better now at supporting him as he wrestles with this severe test of his faith.

Yes, listening *will involve probing for understanding.*
But we have to learn <u>*the difference between:*</u>

- *Thoughtless curiosity* – *"Like one who takes a dog by the ears is he who passes by and meddles with strife not belonging to him."* **Proverbs 26:17**
- *Playing spiritual detective* – There is something about "digging around" in a traumatized soul that tends to make a person feel *unsafe*, and to reinforce the barriers.
- *Canned psychological questions used for effect* – Asking questions that seem clever, or knowledgeable, or "penetrating" to us might make us feel wise or skillful; but it does nothing for the soul of the spiritually struggling warrior, and simply exposes our insincerity.
- *Canned Scriptural platitudes* – This is one of the most common and unhelpful things we (probably all) tend to do. And yet, as obviously unhelpful as it sounds, it's hard to nail down a brief description or example because surely none of us would do such a thing with insincere intent.

Perhaps, in our "faith" that is untested by war we forget that the traumatized warrior may already *know* what we know, and that it is this very "knowledge" that is now being tested as never before by the evils of war. To confidently restate the truth that is now at the core of his fearful questioning will certainly not lead to peace and recovery.

This may be similar to what happens in the soul of believing parents who lose a child. For us to insensitively restate to them truth they already know about having faith in God, will be received by them as further criticism or judgment.

And:

• *Genuine desire to know the person and help him carry his burden.* As I mentioned above, my Marine CPL friend, recently separated from active service, told me that he and his friends had been given business cards, phone numbers and other contact information for post-combat support, but that most of them didn't take advantage of any of it. He said, "You're the only one I've talked to, because you're the only one who really knows me and has gone through so much with me."

Warriors in deep emotional and spiritual pain will eventually respond to true, trustworthy, loving care; *but thoughtless effort and mere technique runs off them like water off of a hard, dry desert.*

Walk with me now through one story of how God fruitfully used His Word, when it was applied to the warrior's soul with timeliness and understanding.

In **Philippians 3:4-21** the Apostle Paul tells his own story of redemption. It was this familiar personal story of the transformation of Saul of Tarsus into the Apostle Paul that God used to provide a foundation for hope and healing for my warrior friend. This took place as he was led, under the guidance of the Spirit, to draw meaning from it *for his own story of brokenness.*

This story is of my believing Marine warrior friend — one of the best of warriors — who became so good at this job of making war, so recognized, admired and awarded, that he came to define himself by the action of war and the personal power and status he had gained.

After separation from active service, he was working through a variety of post-traumatic issues, and now as a follower of Christ he had found this self-definition a *barrier* to progress in healing. He was becoming weary of his unrelenting combative state of mind. He put it to me like this: "If I'm walking down the street and I pass another man, I automatically begin to think about how I would 'take him out.'" This created a *new conflict in his soul*, because as a warrior he had "finally found something he was good at."

At home...prior to enlistment in the Corps, prior to these extreme accomplishments, prior to the sense of power and self-respect they brought, he says he had never been good at anything he did. Despite being a professing believer, his life was empty, purposeless, and even sometimes entangled with the law.

*So letting go of this new life of respect and power as a warrior to rejoin the civilian world **seemed an impossible voluntary return to failure and emptiness.***

As we talked together, we realized that he not only feared the emptiness, and being unknown; but he had also subtly and unintentionally begun to despise the "triviality" of civilian living. When you've been in a life-and-death struggle on behalf of your country, and have been better at it than most, how does anything your civilian acquaintances are doing compare with it in importance? And yet, during the week we spent together, *God finally helped him face the realization that war is not the meaning and purpose of life.*

How could noncombatants grasp the feelings of **disappointment** and **danger** this realization brought to him?

Then, borne out of this *disappointment* and *fear of meaninglessness,* God led us to consider the story of Saul of Tarsus. A man zealous for God, at the top of his game, with the power of life and death over the "enemy." Saul's extreme religious training and knowledge of the Hebrew Scriptures was not a bad thing...what would we in the Church have done without it? Similarly, my warrior friend's combat training and experience were not a bad thing in their appropriate time and place...what would we civilians have done without it?

But when Christ confronted him, Saul realized that he had considered his heritage, his extreme training, and his power to be for his own benefit and selfish purposes.

Saul of Tarsus had to die. He had to become merely "Paul," *a man of dangerous reputation and no future but suffering for the Name of Christ. If he would never be respected or feared again...so be it!* He would count all things to be loss in view of the surpassing value of knowing Christ Jesus his Lord, for Whom he had suffered the loss of all things, and counted them but rubbish so that he might gain Christ.

A true warrior can learn to overcome stress, tension, and painful memories. But to be re-defined from the best at his job to "nobody" but a stressed and potentially dangerous person... *this adds a **new spiritual trauma** to all the traumas of war*. This will take a *surrender* — a word that's been carefully purged from the warrior's vocabulary.

However, my friend consciously grasped and embraced the example of Saul's transformation. Then he returned home, to face the daily post-deployment issues and application of this transformational truth...but now with a *mind* that had been *"re-formed"* by the Spirit of God.

I prayed that, having received Words from God — however familiar — that are truly relevant to his need, my warrior friend would embrace his future simply as a man God would powerfully *remake* in His own *image* and *purpose*. I prayed that this would also help him, little by little, to let down the glass wall surrounding his heart and increasingly open himself to reach out to non-combatants with Christ's love.

I'm sure that not all warriors experience this particular soul conflict...although there may be a significant number of them…probably primarily among those in the Special Operations community who prepare themselves and define themselves as elite warriors.

So please understand that I share this story of my warrior friend as an example of *listening from the heart and trying to discover, together, words from God that are truly relevant to the individual warrior's need.*

God has confirmed this by what has followed in my friend's life. I don't want to make the outcome of this event seem too easy or magical, as a chaplain friend cautioned me. This warrior has had to hammer out the daily post-combat realities with God. But a few weeks after the events described above, I received a phone call from him. He reported that he had begun to let down the "glass wall" just a little. He began by reluctantly taking the risk of attending part of a church-men's retreat…not the overnight camping part! He didn't feel a need for any more "camp-outs." But he attended the day meetings. During the retreat, he met a man who was mature and sensitive enough that he was able to build a connection with him. This led to further contacts with other men in the church, and he was beginning to attend Bible studies, where he was slowly and cautiously building other relationships.

He has a growing peace in relationships with civilians, who will never know, understand, *or care* what he has gone through…what he is *becoming. Like Paul, he's becoming a new man, allowing God to re-define who and what this man will be.*

Out of this growing relational strength, he also began to re-open his heart to the possibility of female relationships. This may have been the most stressful effort at relational involvement because of the remaining characteristics of combat in his spirit, such as abruptness, impatience with triviality, angry feelings, unintentional coarseness, and being overbearing. Gradually, God led him into relationship...and then into marriage...with a godly young woman who, as a Christian college grad, is mature enough to "see through" the lingering issues and love him as the man he is becoming. This process has obviously taken a few years, with plenty of challenges and setbacks. *But it began with the mutual discovery of biblical truth that was truly suitable to his unique post-combat issues.*

12.

THE POWER OF WORDS

I nteraction with warriors has led me to believe we need to explore more deeply the words, *"LOVE,"* "COMFORT," *"FORGIVENESS," and "SPIRITUALITY,"* as they relate to a warrior's experience in combat, and to our use of these words in attempting to help with the healing and restoration process.

All four words are common in our vocabulary of support and healing. Sometimes I wonder whether they may be too common. Perhaps the *ways we use them* are too common and familiar.

This familiarity may cause us to lose sight of the huge variety of meanings and applications of the words, and also of the vast difference between the theoretical knowledge of them and the warrior's real understanding and experience of them.

LOVE

In seeking to minister to combatants, this important dimension of their warrior life has come into a new light for me and plays a vital role in my understanding. It holds real potential in contribution to their soul healing.

The meaning and power of the "brother love" that warriors — especially young infantrymen — experience in life-and-death combat has become a frequent theme in books, movies, and everyday conversations. This has led to a popular awareness of a special bond that forms among men and women who live and operate in life-threatening situations and depend utterly on one another for survival.

The intensity of this sense of life-and-death brotherhood was refreshed for me just today as I heard a "Tier one" Special Operator's reaction when someone compared this warrior's love for his brothers to that of the most elite professional athletes on the football field. I'll give a rough paraphrase here of what this warrior said.

"We're not on a football field entertaining an audience for fame and money. This is a brotherhood forged in war, in the face of death, without recognition, on orders from the people and leaders of our nation."

As I mentioned from Junger's book earlier, common interests, personal beliefs, ethnicity, personality differences, educational background…none of these things has any conscious meaning to the warrior in a firefight or a freezing recon hide-site. Only the mutual assurance that "I will give my life if necessary, to save 'my brother's,' and he will do the same for me," has meaning in that deadly world. (A Marine SGT asked me, "What would people think if they saw two Marines huddled together in one sleeping bag trying to stay warm?") This is a reality in the warrior's life that few non-combatants will ever experience. It's probably the reason that biblical "critics" have made smirking allusions to the brother love of David and Jonathan, and Bible expositors have sometimes stumbled over understanding and explaining it. And yet, what David and Jonathan experienced seems to have been very much like what we witness among warriors today, or in any generation.

This "brother love" may be for the warrior a kind of limited realization of the self-giving, unconditional love we all long for and seldom find or give to others in our busy, self-serving lives.

In this sense it is for them a tantalizing taste of the true love of God in Christ, which perhaps few of these young warriors have felt, even in the church contexts they experienced in their childhood. Considering this, it can serve as a window into the soul of the warrior and an analogy for helping him understand the love of Christ.

Look again at David and Jonathan, in 1 Samuel chapters 13-14. Saul's son, Jonathan, is introduced to us as a warrior, the equivalent of an Infantry Battalion Commander, in charge of 1,000 men. He leads from the front and his courage and aggressiveness are demonstrated in 14:1-15 where, accompanied only by his armor bearer, he assaults the garrison of the Philistines, running forward about three miles and climbing precipitous walls of craggy rock... to attack a high stronghold from an inferior position.

Following this, 1 Samuel 18:1 tells us, "Now it came about when he had finished speaking to Saul, that the soul of Jonathan was knit to the soul of David, and Jonathan loved him as himself." In 19:1 we're told, "...Jonathan, Saul's son, greatly delighted in David."

This was a life-and-death situation for all involved. Saul was at war with the Philistines, David's life was on the line daily as he faithfully fought Saul's battles, and then again when he dared to return to Saul's demented presence. Jonathan was fighting the Philistines with David, and simultaneously fighting for David's life in the face of his own deranged father.

Finally, in 2 Samuel 1:5-17, the deaths in battle of Saul and Jonathan are reported to David and a soul-searing battlefield memorial service is held as he "...chants with his lament over Saul and Jonathan his son."

This love that goes out, not once, but day-after-day into the face of death, unhesitatingly to lay its life down for its brother is not familiar to us as non-combatants. **But it exists... no...*it is an essential element of the warrior's existence***

In his book, *War,* Sebastian Junger has a chapter titled, "LOVE." He begins the chapter with a quote from J. Glenn Gary's book, *The Warriors,* in which Gary says, *"The coward's fear of death stems in large part from his incapacity to love anything but his own body."* Because of this he can't develop any inner resources sufficient to overcome the terror of death.

In this chapter, Junger describes a situation where a soldier took an AK-47 round directly to his helmet. The bullet was stopped and he later returned to the fight. The greater trauma was to his team leader, who *had promised his guys that none of them would die.*

In his sincere and determined love for his men, he assured them he would take care of them...that they didn't need to worry, they would be going home to their girlfriends, moms, dads. The round that struck his soldier's helmet *struck him* with the reality that he *might not be able* to keep his men from being hurt or killed. He found himself sitting, trembling, and thinking that the worst possible thing would be to be in charge of someone's life...and then to lose him! *He simply could not imagine that day.*

My Marine Special Operations friend was a Team Leader, and while he was at home recovering from injuries, some of the men on his team in Afghanistan had been injured and one was killed. When he read the words above he said, "That's exactly how I felt!"

Further along, Junger notes what he says some Army psychologists have come to understand: that **courage is love.** He says, *"In war, neither could exist without the other, and...in a sense they were just different ways of saying the same thing."*

Junger closes his chapter on "Love" with an insight we must try to take hold of if we wish to touch the hearts of combatants.

He concludes that in combat, mutual defense can become so consuming it becomes the group's very reason for existence. He believes that every man at Restrepo outpost secretly wished the enemy would make a serious effort at overrunning them. Though it would be a nightmare event, it would be the ultimate proof of their *bond and fighting ability*. After re-deploying to their home Post in Vicenza, Italy, he asked a soldier if he missed Restrepo. The soldier replied that he'd take a helicopter there tomorrow, and he was sure most of the men felt the same.

What this warrior *did not* understand is that Restrepo represented something unique — a *bond of love* that could not be reproduced by going back. Everything would have been different...would have proven disappointing and disorienting. *It would have been something like going home, where he would find himself alone, his brothers scattered to the four winds, all of them left to fight alone their private personal battles with post-traumatic issues...without that love.*

In his book, *Shadow Of The Sword...* Marine SSGT Jeremiah Workman talks about missing his "brothers," wishing they could have all stayed together. But then he realized that it could never be the same again. Having returned to the U.S. and his unit split up by the Corps, he saw that he was now living among "strangers in uniform, men and women who didn't have our frame of reference." He says that after months of combat they had become a family...well, he acknowledges, it was a "dysfunctional family with guns and a disgusting sense of humor."

No matter how the warrior yearns for what he had in war, he can't go back. *But the life-sacrificing love he experienced in battle remains for him a memory and a standard he clings to*...a way of reassuring himself that no matter how tough the post-war battle becomes, no matter how lonely and isolated he feels among "the normals," somewhere there are a few friends who "have been there," who would understand him.

In his comments below, Chaplain Mike Hoyt shows us more of the complexity of this longing to "go back" and how in the heart of the warrior it defines itself down to "brother love."

"Danger (war or threatening circumstance, like extreme military training environments) produces a heightened sense of awareness of the events and impacts of the experiences lived through under those conditions. The emotions are stamped deeper and more permanently than at any other time. That is why persons often at risk describe their experience as 'when I felt really alive!' The point is, soldiers are left with a lot of 'residuals'; with overwhelming emotional markers carved into their being and soul. Returning to Restrepo is tied to several issues competing for jurisdiction. (First) a desire to return to

that sensory rush of heightened awareness (more than an adrenaline thing, this is about being in contact with the essence of the great paradox: fragility and conquest). Second, the need to re-create the effect of belonging to a mission and purpose compelling and larger than one's self yet intertwined in a corporate outcome. Third, the desire to believe one is valued and making a critical difference, something akin to teamwork but not always dependent on people. The last residual, a degree of mutual accountability. This fosters the aspect of self-sacrifice, heroism, communal suffering or shared extreme effort under hardships, depravity, danger. The feelings, emotions, decisions animating all of the above are also caught up in one's apprehension of the meaning of "love." Love of Country, purpose, buddy, excitement, contribution, survival, competition, and sometimes love of God; but the last one is hard to figure in war. For a young, impressionable, untutored heart the residuals are often too much to bear. So, love gets reinterpreted into a bunch of spasmodic "quick fixes" that address residual symptoms with no coherent framework to set things right or understand love in a broad context of loss-grief-survival-sacrifice-thrill-value-meaning. You are absolutely right on the target with your words: (see below) *'misunderstands, grasping behaviors, unsatisfied, substitutes.' However, the up-front answer is not a Bible study or a scripture walk or even reli-gious concepts...it is EXACTLY what you say below: We get that awareness by first listening with hearing ears and knowing the warrior. One must know the military mind-set you so rightly acknowledge, and accept their version of love, in all its unfinished and incomplete forms from danger and war, and move out gently to a rendezvous with the True love of God, His Good Shepherd who lays down His life for the sheep."*

When we say to the warrior, "God loves you and will be with you," we may be unknowingly creating in the warrior's mind an implied *contrast* between the love of *the unseen God* and the love of a brother who fights beside him, *visibly* laying down his own life for his protection. On the other hand, **with God's wisdom, we can help him perceive the invisible but perfect love of God, by means of the visible and recognizable love of a brother**...as Mike says, to help them, **"move out gently to a rendezvous with the true love of God, His Good Shepherd Who lays down His life for the sheep."**

Perhaps it is *this Friend* the writer of Proverbs 18:24 *ultimately* had in mind when he said, "A man of many friends may come to ruin, but there is a friend who sticks closer than a brother."

We need to be as aware as possible of the mind-set on which our words of love are landing. We gain that awareness by first listening with hearing ears and knowing the warrior.

185

His war-trained mindset about love *doesn't have to be* an obstacle or a source of confusion. *It can become a bridge* for him to understand the self-sacrificial Love of Christ that transcends the greatest "brother love" he's experienced in war.

Constructing that bridge is a sensitive task, to be done with thoughtfulness. This includes the necessary awareness of **an *additional background influence*** *that was active in preparing the warrior to believe that this "brother love" is the real...the ultimate...thing.*

As I said earlier, once again, we have to sadly acknowledge that many — perhaps most — of our young infantrymen come from troubled backgrounds. There was undoubtedly some religious experience, but *many were deprived of the quality of parental, or other adult, influence that allowed them to feel loved and valued unconditionally.*

And so they approach their military training with a void of this kind of love in their hearts. This is the ideal spiritual medium in which the transforming work of their basic and advanced combat training does its work. The goal of basic military training, especially for the combat MOSs, is to erase the civilian and create the warrior...one who is now *accepted* and *initiated* into a *special brotherhood*...where he has *proven himself trustworthy and valuable to his brothers.*

Furthermore, the course of his training has been supplemented with emotionally powerful *symbols* and *images* of the uniqueness of this "band of brothers." To try to convey the depth and importance of this initiation and commitment, at least one author I've read has compared this process to a young man being initiated into a gang. *Now all that's needed is to add war!* In life-and-death battle this already-established brotherhood, this mutual commitment to protect one another at all costs, <u>*becomes*</u> *a form of love that he's never experienced before*...a love that surpasses all others he can comprehend.

So our war-traumatized friend comes to us with a conviction that he has experienced unique and unconditional love in combat. And yet in his heart he knows this love is fragile, because he also *knows* his "brothers" at another human level, and he *feels* this love beginning to break down as the brotherhood is separated from combat and from one another.

This exposes one of the *complications*, and also *opportunities*, presented by the experience of extreme "brother love." *It is the tendency of the traumatized warrior to seek support and validation through post-combat connections with war buddies.*

He longs to be with those who have demonstrated the love that would give its life for him. But now, in his post-combat loneliness and isolation, *he misunderstands...*

In his attempts to resurrect that "brother love," with the rest of his friends *he substitutes the destructive peripheral behaviors he has experienced with his comrades*, like drinking and partying together.

It doesn't work. He doesn't understand that *it wasn't the trappings*, but *the dying for one another* that created the love.

His attempts to recreate the love without the war leave him *unsatisfied, repeating the behavior, grasping for what he'll never find down this path. There's no love there.*

But here we may find that bridge to real hope for him. If we can see beyond our own self-protective, theoretical versions of love, and draw *new understanding for ourselves* from his life-transforming experience, then perhaps we'll be able to guide him into true knowledge of **the *One Who is* the Love** *that all other loves seek to emulate.*

God grant us wisdom to guide the warrior to the supreme, self-sacrificing, redeeming love of Christ that won't leave him empty and comfortless when his warrior brothers are deployed forward without him, discharged, reassigned, and scattered to the four winds. This is the love that truly understands what he's been through, and the soul damage he's suffering today, because:

"...we do not have a high priest who cannot sympathize with our weaknesses, but One who has been tempted in all things as we are, yet without sin." Hebrews 4:15

"...and He Himself bore our sins in His body on the cross, so that we might die to sin and live to righteousness; for by His wounds you were healed." 1Peter 2:24

"For it was fitting for Him, for whom are all things, and through whom are all things, in bringing many sons to glory, to perfect the author of their salvation through sufferings." Hebrews 2:10

For most of us, throughout our lives those crushing realities of Jesus' experience have been wonderful theological truths. *For the soul-traumatized warrior they are the core of his hope, the emotional breeching charge that can open his heart to ultimate love and healing.* In my meditations in Matthew 26:1-46 on the horrible hours Jesus spent during His last Passover and in Gethsemane, I've been more overwhelmed than ever before with the depth of His love. ***Jesus is facing a form and depth of grief and sorrow that no other man has ever faced, and He's facing it absolutely alone.*** No one else could possibly understand what He was preparing to take upon Himself...not only excruciating pain and physical suffering, but the *blame* for all our sins and the *shame* of all our guilt...*this Man Who is guilty of none of it.*

I think that if we can take a soul-damaged warrior into these hours in Gethsemane and help him walk through them with Jesus, he'll be able to find hope in the Person who <u>has</u> been *"touched with the feeling of his infirmities" and loved his unworthy soul enough to die in his place.*

At this time in Gethsemane, Jesus is within two days of His death, and several days ago he began His move toward His ultimate battle space on earth, His own chosen and lovingly cultivated city, Jerusalem, that has been overrun by the *religiously corrupt* opposing force of the enemy. He's been telling His disciples that this is the culmination of His mission on earth that has been battle-planned from eternity past.

Since He arrived in the city, He has been *consciously confronting and provoking the religious enemy*, and now He knows the ambush is being laid for Him. In verse 2 He says to His followers, "you know that after two days the Passover is coming." Of course they knew it! The place was a madhouse of pilgrims and marketing noise.

But He follows this obvious comment with the hard reminder that "The Son of Man *is to be* handed over for crucifixion." The words, *"to be,"* are not in the original language, but are filled in by translators. The original says, "The Son of Man *is handed over* for crucifixion."

When I noticed this form of wording, I began to perceive it more accurately for what it actually was, the final briefing before launching the assault on the enemy's stronghold with the assured result of His own death. I can hear Him saying, "Remember now, *this is how this thing goes down.... don't forget the plan, and get yourselves ready."* I feel I can almost hear Him follow these words with, "Alright, let's do it!" In fact these are almost the very words He used. In verse 46 He says, *get up, let's go, the one who betrays me is here.*

He knew that at this very moment the chief priests and elders were already gathered in ambush, and the traitor was ready to slip out and sell Jesus to them.

Except for His Father in Heaven, no one could possibly understand Jesus' horrible aloneness, His suffering, His sacrifice, His lifting onto His own back the terrible "ruck"

*of our sins and failures that was impossible for us to carry,
ourselves.*

He drew a few of His closest followers aside with Him for
His final time of prayer and then gave Himself to facing the
battle ahead. He told His friends that His grief was as deep as
death itself and Luke 22:44 says, *"...being in agony He was
praying very fervently; and His sweat became like drops of
blood falling down upon the ground."*

His most loyal friends, still unable to grasp the depth of
His grief and aloneness, couldn't so much as stay awake with
Him. They dozed as He pled with His Father to allow this
"assignment" to pass Him by if possible.

*Then, with no friend who understood what His soul was
suffering, absolutely alone*, except for His Father's presence,
He accepted His Father's will.

If the warrior we are caring for feels alone, isolated from
everyone — even from his own family — if he feels misun-
derstood and hopeless...then we need to help him consider
the MAN, who at such great cost has already picked up the
warrior's load and carried it for him. He can trade his unbearable load of loneliness, pain, and confusion for a "yoke that
is easy and a burden that is light," if he will turn to this MAN
for understanding, forgiveness, and comfort.

**But, hold on for a moment. There is still *another*
perspective we need to be aware of on this "brother love"
among warriors theme.**

I continue as often as possible to pass what I write by the warriors themselves for their comments, corrections, and guidance. Recently, by way of my Intel Colonel's referral, I received a response from an Air Force Special Operations warrior with six combat deployments behind him and another to come in a few months.

His comments about combat "brother love" were a strong reminder that we must *hear the warrior*, and not presume it's all the same for everyone.

One might assume that tight-knit Special Operations teams would experience this bond of love above all else. But this warrior's contrasting experience corresponds to that which an Army SF officer has also shared with me in the past.

Here are his words:

"Love is my motivation. A guy like me that never fights with those I train with, it's sometimes hard for me to 'feel the Love' with the team I'm with. I cherish the deployments when it is there. There's one team I was with where I had to 'earn my way in.' That was one of my proudest deployments when I was able to prove myself and my worth to them under fire. There (have) been a couple other deployments where it came easy, and I fit right in. Again, those were good deployments. One sticks out in my mind, where I never did fit in with the team. All I could do is just bear down and do the best I could. It's good when there is Love and respect

between each other on the battlefield. But when there's not, I lean on my love for my family, my country, and my God for motivation."

Even in this very poignant personal example, one thing that comes through clearly is that love is a dominant theme in the heart of a warrior in combat. Since God Himself is the only source of unfailing love, and since the need and longing for it is so amplified in the context of combat, we sense even more urgently the need to lead our warriors to its *Source*.

I think these war-generated expressions of love, and the longing for it, may be used as "redemptive analogies," such as missionaries have looked for in tribal cultures around the world *to point the warrior to the ultimate Source of love and redemption.*

COMFORT

This is a wonderfully nuanced concept. Our attempts to provide it for another person can prove to be everything from effective and encouraging to distracting and even irritating. This is especially true of our efforts with combatants because of the intensity, and "otherness" of their experience. Feel with me the power of the words of the AF Special Operator I quoted above. He begins his comments on this topic of comfort with the words:

"There is no comfort in war. A true warrior knows that. That's why it's important for warriors to feel the appreciation for the sacrifices made during a time of war."

In other words, for him, "comfort" begins with being valued.

We must consider carefully *how* to *value* a soldier who's already traumatized and is now headed back to war after his R&R or into a new deployment. He may be returning to nightly patrols, knowing from past experience that the patrol will be hit every night by at least one IED and there is a high probability he will be killed or maimed tonight, or tomorrow night, or some night in the near future.

One of the things we need to discern is that ministering comfort to a warrior who is *going into combat*, and one dealing with *post*-traumatic issues are quite different matters.

*The comfort of loving, appreciative, non-judgmental **personal presence** is powerful in the face of almost any kind of suffering.* We can offer this to a wounded or traumatized warrior if we are physically nearby, or even by telephone where possible. However, in the attempt to help a warrior overcome combat trauma, *this comfort-of-presence is only the beginning.* It provides the *tone* of the relationship, but w*ords will eventually be called for, first by the hurting warrior when he's ready to talk, and then meaningful words of* *comfort and hope by his friend*, with growing understanding and *appropriate* biblical guidance.

This highlights another important point we have to address for those we serve. *We can only offer meaningful comfort if it is accompanied by the impartation of* **hope**. *But we must first discover* **what hope looks like** *at any given moment, in any individual warrior's life.*

For example, if our warrior friend has not yet "understood the grace of God in truth," received the hope laid up in heaven for him through Christ, and been "rescued from the domain of darkness and transferred to the kingdom of God's beloved Son" (Colossians 1), *then the impartation of this* **eternal hope** will be the **beginning of comfort** for his soul as he steps out knowing that his next few steps could carry him into eternity.

If he is a believer, dealing with the residual terror of combat, shame, guilt, or some painful loss, the path to revived hope in God will look different.

There is important guidance for ministering comfort to a wounded warrior in Scotty Smiley's book, *Hope Unseen,* as he shares how God walked him through the process of healing his soul. (This is a book I'll be sharing with troubled warriors at every appropriate opportunity.)

CPT Smiley is a West Point educated, Ranger trained, Infantry Platoon leader who was totally blinded by a VBIED (Vehicle Borne IED) during combat in Iraq. He was raised in a Christian family and approached war with a strong personal faith in Christ. His faith itself was severely damaged by the loss of his eyesight, and chapter-by-chapter he reveals the healing work of God.

Following are thoughts I've drawn from what he has shared in the book, including the selected scripture passages and quotations that God used in his life, which are instructive for those of us seeking to help soul-damaged warriors.

In Chapter One, Scotty is *reflecting on a moment early in his healing process.* He tells how two years earlier, three months after losing the use of his eyes, he had hit bottom in his struggle to believe that God was still God. By now, at the time of his reflections, he had regained his trust that the God who loved him before the injury was the same God who loved him still. But this restoration of hope had only come after he had found himself crumpled on a cement slab near the V.A. Blind Rehabilitation Center, pleading to know "who he was" now, and trying to understand what God wanted from him.

Scotty heads Chapter Four with this quote from Psalm 40:

"I waited patiently for the Lord; and He inclined to me and heard my cry. He brought me up out of the pit of destruction, out of the miry clay. And He set my feet upon a rock, making my footsteps firm. He put a new song in my mouth, a song of praise to our God;"

He heads Chapter Ten with Psalm 34:18:

"The Lord is near to the brokenhearted and saves those who are crushed in spirit."

His memory of waking from a coma with his dad nearby will undoubtedly resonate with many damaged young Infantrymen and help us understand the unspoken shame they feel. Now his dad stood over him in his hospital bed at Walter Reed to kiss him and tell him he loved him, *and what Scotty felt was embarrassment and shame at being an imperfect soldier.*

This is where he tells of that broken moment I mentioned earlier, when his friends' singing and laughing in their well-meaning efforts to give comfort, actually made him feel ill as he lay there, overwhelmed with anger, feeling betrayed by God.

He understood and forgave his family and friends; but he felt his sanity attacked by the circus of happy traffic in his room. These people weren't blind...weren't living his life. He reports that he felt guilt for questioning God as he did, but "what you believe can change when your world is blown apart." He didn't even want to pray any more. But then he heads Chapter Fourteen with Mark 9:24:

"Immediately the boy's father cried out, and said 'I do believe; help my unbelief.'"

Later, he reveals another important means God used to help in his warrior soul's restoration. In this case it was the

simple words of inspiration and encouragement of a significant friend who assured him and his wife that he'd be holding
on for them, watching to see what God had in store for the
rest of their lives; and he assured them of his confidence that
it would be good.

The **right words** of **value** from the **right person** at the
right time can have surprising power.

Near the end of his book, Scotty shares his bottom-line
statement of faith. Not just anyone would be welcomed in
saying these words to a broken warrior, but perhaps we can
"be Scotty" to our warrior friend by humbly quoting his words
at the right moment as he says:

> *"Every day I must choose to embrace the life He gave
> me. The first thing I will see when I get to heaven is
> Christ's face. That gets me through the hard times."*

He concludes his book with the words of a Jeremy Camp
song, "This life is not the finish line," and he confesses that
although he has doubted at times, God has picked him up and
continues to guide him step-by-step.

To this faithful testimony by Scotty, Chaplain Mike Hoyt
offers a quotation from 2 Corinthians 1:3-4:

> *"Blessed be the God and Father of our Lord Jesus
> Christ, the father of mercies and God of all comfort,
> Who comforts us in all our affliction so that we will*

be able to comfort those who are in any affliction with the comfort with which we ourselves are comforted by God."

Regarding this reference to God's comfort, Mike adds:

"Comfort must be felt and received to be well given. Those of us without the loss and pain of wounded warriors cannot hope to offer God's comfort if we ourselves have not been 'equally broken, destitute,' abhorrent of our position outside of Christ. Everyone cannot go to the battlefield but everyone can and should know the loss of self, the heap of soul 'on the cement pad' before God and never forget that humbled-wretched-hopeless spot. Only from there can we give comfort...be the comfort...with 'which we ourselves are comforted by God.' This is not sweet, simple, positive attitude, optimistic happy face hospital or counseling room stuff. This is recovery-based comfort from a grimy, beggarly life that understands mercy, need, and redemption."

FORGIVENESS

It's hard to know where to start this sensitive, complex subject regarding our damaged warriors. My mind is flooded with thoughts, conflicts, and puzzles growing out of the experiences and words of combatants.

Maybe the best place to start is by repeating a quote I shared above from my friend, an Army Intelligence Colonel, in his Veteran's Day message. It was his comment that forced me to recognize the "problem" of forgiveness for combatants.

> *"There is a point where no matter how righteous or warranted the kill, no matter how evil the foe, there is a point where it is too much. I am not trying to sound unpatriotic; I am very patriotic. I am just trying to explain how some of those soldiers at the extreme edge carry a different burden than others.*

> *"One friend told me, 'I signed up to defend my country, not to kill, and kill, and kill.' Another said,* **'I don't want to be thanked, I want to be forgiven.'** *A big problem is, those that feel the most that way, will never say a word. They are too ashamed. They will never acknowledge they have killed anyone much less 40 or 50."*

My friend followed by saying, *"That's the way I feel, too."* He has been a believer for many years, has studied the Bible, and has received excellent Bible teaching from a variety of sources. He could readily articulate a theologically sound explanation of the atoning death of Christ, His imputed righteousness to repentant believers, and *His forgiveness of the most wicked sinners.*

Then how can it be that he and so many other combatants who know and believe this truth, still find themselves at times unable to experience a deep, peace-imparting **sense** *of forgiveness?* How can it be that warriors who belong by faith to the Lord Jesus are "sentenced" to go on with their lives day-after-day, believing — and yet somehow lacking assurance — that they have been fully and truly forgiven by the mercy and grace of the sovereign Judge of the universe? This experience is not unique to American warriors. I'm sure it is a burden borne by believing warriors in any age, culture, or society. This is movingly illustrated in an article written by an OMF International missionary in Cambodia. The website and attribution information is in the selected reading bibliography at the back of the book. By permission, here is a quotation from the article:

Will God Forgive?
By Nathan Martin
From 1975-1979, an estimated 2 million people were killed in Cambodia under Pol Pot's harsh Khmer Rouge regime. The scars from that time remain in the country today. Below is a story of a former soldier and his struggle to accept God's grace and forgiveness.
April 2012

One of our top priorities right now is to disciple the members of the small worship group that meets in the nearby village of Snuol Leitch. At times, it feels like the group is hanging by a thread, but we know behind the scenes it continues by the grace of God.

Daniel and I meet weekly with Sann, the man who leads the group, to reflect together on a Bible passage in preparation for Sunday. Recently, we read in Matthew 5 from Jesus' Sermon on the Mount where Jesus says not only those who kill, but also those who are angry and say evil things about others, are in danger of judgment.

In the first read through, Sann fell asleep while reading out loud. "It's going to be a long afternoon," I thought to myself. We read it again and Sann asked me to explain, saying "I don't understand any of it."

I did some basic teaching on Jesus not just looking at our outward actions, but also at our heart when it comes to judging sin. We talked more about sin and our resulting need for forgiveness through Jesus Christ. After reading the passage again, Sann asked, "Does Christ's forgiveness cover sins you don't know are sins?"

Good question. We talked more, affirming that, yes, Christ paid it all on the cross. Then Sann asked, "What about soldiers who shoot and kill people? Will Christ forgive them?" At this point, I had no idea where Sann was going with this. Yes, Christ will surely forgive if they believe. Sann continued, "What if during Pol Pot somebody shot and killed several people ..."

Daniel got it before I did. Sann wasn't talking hypothetically; he was talking about himself. Sann then told us the story in detail, of him running and crying later, and of being afraid to talk to God about what he did, even though he has been a believer for several years now.

Reading the Bible with Sann the past couple of weeks has been a struggle. But it was an amazing blessing to see the Holy Spirit go far beyond anything I had planned and use this text to cut Sann to the heart and bring healing where there was doubt and pain. The good news is that yes, the cross is sufficient to pay it all. Yes, even murderers (in body, heart or tongue) can have all the dirt washed clean at the cross. Thanks be to God through Jesus Christ!

We ended with Sann offering up this pain and doubt in his heart to Christ in prayer, then clapping his hands in joy at this new, deeper understanding of the radical goodness of his Savior.

Perhaps it will also help the warrior you're caring for to know that this soul pain of *unfelt forgiveness* is *not unique to combatants*. It seems that, regardless how "good" or "bad" any of us have been, *the more we realize the ugliness of our sin in the presence of a holy God, the more unworthy we feel of His forgiveness.* Surely this must be amplified immensely in the heart of one who has shed much blood in war.

Again, it's hard to know which of many ways to go next in considering this. So I'll just launch into the thoughts that are on my mind, and hope that we as Christian servants can compassionately draw out increasing help and peace for the hearts of our warriors.

I'll start by simply laying out the obvious question: *When we have already consciously embraced the truth of Romans 8:1 that God's justice was fully met in Christ, and "...there is now no condemnation for those who are in Christ Jesus," why does increased or sudden awareness of our badness and unworthiness lead to the feeling of not being forgiven?*

In *non-combatants* I think it's often actually the result of growing in the knowledge of God...growing from an early, shallow sense of our sinfulness to the searing awareness of His unapproachable purity. *I know this is true in my own life.*

The closer I draw to Him, the more urgently I'm driven back again to seek the assurances in His Word that my forgiveness and acceptance by God are not based on the slightest shred of worthiness in me, but on the worthiness of Jesus alone. He, knowing everything about me, past, present, and future has covered my wretchedness with His own blood, and imputed to my unworthy account His own perfect righteousness.

If I'm correct in believing that this feeling of unforgiveness *for non-combatants* is actually borne of *growth in awareness of our unworthiness*, then we must also acknowledge that in our case we have the "luxury" of having it revealed to us at the chosen pace of our own study and meditation.

What must it be like for the warrior who, in combat, is suddenly slammed face-to-face with the abject evil of humanity, both the enemy's and his own? This didn't take place in the safety of his prayer room or office, where he can quickly turn to the Word for reassurance…or even choose to defer facing it until a time and place when he feels safer in dealing with it.

No, in his case this internal moral confrontation might have begun in a deadly, confusing firefight; or in a raging vengeful retaliation after friends had been killed by and IED; or watching as an enemy died a slow suffering death; or being the one to send "his boys" on a patrol that led to their harm in an ambush; or finding himself wishing everyone of the same race of his enemy were dead; or even *all* the above strung out over multiple deployments.

He didn't have the opportunity to choose a comfortable time, place, and pace for facing and acknowledging the devastating extremity of his unworthiness of God's forgiveness. His vile sinfulness (which is no worse than my own) and it's immeasurable contrast to God's infinite holiness has simply been shoved in his face along with plenty of unforgettable images, sounds, and smells to remind him every day and night of why he "should never be forgiven."

Surely all of us will be able to see what "strangers" we are to this conflict in his soul, and how sterile our familiar assurances will initially seem to him. But the truth is clear, and only the truth will set him free. So just as surely, we must humbly step onto this battlefield with him and help him overcome this weapon of the enemy...the *lie* that he is not — or cannot be — forgiven.

It's uncomfortable to bring up the further thoughts that I think need to be considered about this. But I believe it's necessary to meaningfully break through the strong wall of "unworthiness" that hinders full soul healing and restoration of joy.

It's possible that some warriors may be more susceptible to this weapon of the enemy because of a lack of adequate focus on it in their spiritual preparation for war, or a lack of opportunity to develop their understanding.

I've spoken to a lot of young Marines — professing believers — during their time in the School Of Infantry, who were consciously addressing the question of the morality of killing. Most had resolved the question at the most basic level, "Is it wrong to kill someone in the service of my country and under the authority of the command?" It's not difficult for them to arrive at the, "no," answer to this basic question.

But what about the questions they did not adequately address in advance?

What if the question turns out to be, *"Is it wrong if I kill ten, or a hundred?"* Or suppose it turns out to be, *"What if I followed the ROE (Rules of Engagement) and mistakenly killed a carload of people, all family members, who ran up on a mounted patrol and foolishly refused or neglected to stop when repeatedly signaled?"* Or, *"What if I called in artillery on a house full of people and found that my intelligence had been wrong?"*

There's an almost unlimited supply of these kinds of unprepared-for scenarios experienced by our warriors that can lead to the hopeless conviction that what I've done is too terrible to be forgiven.

If we dare to dream of helping the warrior break through this hopeless barrier, *it may require asking him to take some painful medicine in the form of **a hard question**.* This question is useful for any of us who suffer with the feeling that *my* sins are too heinous to be forgiven.

The question is this: ***"Is it possible that to some degree my pride may be playing a part?"*** I *said* it's a hard question; but work with me and perhaps not only our warrior friend, but we ourselves, may be helped.

Let's look at the question in a very practical form:

*"Is it possible that at some deeply hidden level I still imagine that I should **not** be considered so bad that I wouldn't be acceptable to God…that somehow, apart from what war*

*did to me, **I might have been able to be "worthy"** of His forgiveness...that **my** relatively minor sinfulness wouldn't have been a problem for His forgiveness? Maybe, if not for what war did to me, I could have taken His forgiveness in stride without doubting it or feeling too bad about it."*

It's possible that, however consciously or unconsciously, a warrior might *not* believe in the depths of his heart that naked, broken, unworthy repentance before God is *all he could ever have offered Him.*

For any of us, including the warrior, it's possible that by my intelligence, achievements, shrewdness, general good guy nature...fill in the blank...I may be deceived into thinking that *I shouldn't* be caught in this wretchedly uncomfortable place of having done something so terrible that *it made me feel* I couldn't be forgiven. Apart from what war did to me, *I don't think of myself as that bad a person.*

This is the deceitfulness of that original pride about which God says, "The heart is more deceitful than all else and is desperately sick; who can understand it?" Jeremiah 17:9

If a warrior will recognize the deceitfulness of these proud imaginations, confess his utter unworthiness to God war-or-no-war, and cast himself on the <u>adequacy</u> and <u>finality</u> of the judgment God laid on Jesus, it may be the beginning of release from the emotional and spiritual prison of "not feeling worthy to be forgiven."

It's a *contradiction* to imagine that in our sinful human flesh any of us could be "worthy" of God's grace and forgiveness.

May we never diminish the awfulness of our own, or any person's, sin; but God in His kindness has revealed to us in His holy Word the stories of murderers and adulterers, who became not only useful to Him but, as in David's case, a man after God's own heart, *because* "...He is opposed to the proud, but **gives grace** to the humble." James 4:6 The sins in these cases were not made light of, and their temporal consequences were not glossed over. *But forgiveness was complete.*

God lovingly describes His own attitude in Isaiah 57:15-19. It's a long passage to fully include here, but it's too powerfully gracious and important to simply list the reference.

"For thus says the high and exalted One Who lives forever, whose name is Holy, 'I dwell on a high and holy place, and also with the contrite and lowly of spirit in order to revive the spirit of the lowly and revive the heart of the contrite. For I will not contend forever, nor will I always be angry; for the spirit would grow faint before Me, and the breath of those whom I have made. Because of the iniquity of his unjust gain I was angry and struck him; I hid My face and was angry and he went on turning away, in the way of his heart. I have seen his ways, but I will heal him; I will lead him and restore comfort to him and to his mourners, Creating the praise of the lips. Peace, peace to him who is far and to him who is near,' says the Lord, 'and I will heal him.'"

God has made His "perspective" clear in this matter of forgiveness.

In Isaiah 55:7-12, God tells us what He __demands__, and what He __promises__.

His demand — *"Let the wicked forsake his way and the unrighteous man his thoughts; and let him return to the Lord...and to our God..."*

In the case of the troubled warriors God has brought to us, there may or may not be any actual wicked ways or unrighteous thoughts underlying his sense of unforgiveness. Perhaps, our first responsibility will be to help him resolve *that* question. But if some sin or wickedness is truly the hidden power behind his feelings of guilt and rejection, then God can help us mercifully and patiently assist him in forsaking the sin and returning to the Lord and to our God. And God will surely and faithfully honor His promise...

His promise — *"...He will have compassion on him...for He will abundantly pardon."*

Our warrior friend will undoubtedly ask the same question you or I would ask upon recognizing the wretchedness of our sin..."*how can God do this when I think and feel the way I do?"*

God answers: Because,

"...My thoughts are not your thoughts, nor are your ways My ways, declares the Lord. For as the heavens are higher than the earth, so are My ways higher than

your ways and My thoughts than your thoughts. For as the rain and snow come down from heaven, and do not return there without watering the earth and making it bear and sprout...so will My Word be which goes forth from my Mouth; It will not return to me empty without accomplishing what I desire and without succeeding in the matter for which I sent it."

And *what is the matter* for which He will send His Word on behalf of the repentant one? He **promises** that *"..you will go out with joy and be led forth with peace..."*

This promise is not for "good" people but for the *"unrighteous"* and *"wicked."* "Abundant" means His pardon is *more than enough* to cover my wickedness. The praise and thanks go to Jesus-God our Savior!

Further thoughts on hindrances to fully resting in God's forgiveness.

Having faced this foundational truth about "worthiness," *it may yet help us to explore some further thoughts* on what may be behind the *feeling* of unforgiveness.

Perhaps it is:

A lack of true and full repentance.

Perhaps my warrior friend's conduct — whether actual sin is involved or not — *has felt too awful for him to consciously expose it to God.* It makes him sick to think of bringing it up to God and confessing it by name and description. Which of us sinners doesn't know this fear if we've ever been deeply honest with ourselves?

So he tries to keep it hidden even from God, like a child who holds something behind his back, imagining somehow his parent won't see it. In this case there can't be real and deep release, which leaves a void of the *feeling* of forgiveness. But the real and true release is ready to be imparted from the heart of God at the moment the warrior brings his hidden sin to God.

A fear of his "badness" being somehow, somewhere, sometime, <u>exposed to other people</u>, and thus it's constantly hidden in a dark room of his soul, gnawing away at his fearful spirit.

It is God's release or forgiveness he needs, but in his heart he hasn't been set free from the fear that if he's exposed to other people, God's forgiveness is somehow nullified...or, worse, his release or forgiveness by God isn't sufficient, if people should find out and despise him.

Maybe we can best help our warrior friend if we first ask *ourselves* these questions, and then help him ask them of himself:

1. Whose forgiveness and/or approval *really matters to me?* And, if I'm truly clean before God...

2. "What can man do to me?"

Psalm 118:5-9:

"From my distress I called upon the LORD; The LORD answered me and set me in a large place. The LORD is for me; I will not fear; what can man do to me? The LORD is for me among those who help me; therefore I will look with satisfaction on those who hate me. It is better to take refuge in the LORD than to trust in man. It is better to take refuge in the LORD than to trust in princes."

The Apostle Paul then follows on the words of the psalmist, speaking directly to us about our fear of being exposed to others, when we have laid ourselves bare before Him.

Romans 8:31-37:

"What then shall we say to these things? If God is for us, who is against us? He who did not spare His own Son, but delivered Him over for us all, how will He not also with Him freely give us all things? Who will bring a charge against God's elect? God is the one who justifies; who is the one who condemns? Christ Jesus is He who died, yes, rather who was raised, who is at the right hand of God, who also intercedes for us. Who will separate us from the love of Christ? Will tribulation, or distress, or persecution, or famine, or nakedness, or peril, or sword? Just as it is written, 'FOR YOUR SAKE WE ARE BEING PUT TO DEATH ALL DAY

*LONG; WE WERE CONSIDERED AS SHEEP TO
BE SLAUGHTERED.' But in all these things we
overwhelmingly conquer through Him who loved us."*

This will require gaining greater *eternal* perspective. Our warrior friend is willing to die for his buddy in combat. *Is he willing to die to the opinions of men, and rest in the knowledge that he is forgiven by God?*

The impression that if he feels bad enough about his sin, if he hates himself enough for being such a wretch, then he will be worthy of God's forgiveness...this is just a variation of the enemy's lie: that we can be...that we *have to be*...worthy to be forgiven.

In this form, we imagine that we *make ourselves worthy* by loathing ourselves. But down this painful and repetitious road there is certainly no sense of true and final forgiveness. The warrior needs help in understanding that emotional self-punishment is not the same as the godly sorrow that leads to true repentance.

And even godly sorrow *doesn't justify* any of us; it simply causes us to return to God, in Whom alone *true*, *trustworthy*, and *full* forgiveness is found.

There are other hidden things that may contribute to the warrior's *feeling* of unforgiveness. Part of the point here is to again remind ourselves that more deeply *knowing* our warrior friend is the path to truly helping him be set free from this, and every other, post-traumatic spiritual trap of the enemy.

We dishonor God if we despise the full and sufficient price that has already been paid for our sins.

There are key passages in God's Word that will help us and our warrior friend see and understand the **nature and extremity of the price that has already been paid for our, and his, wicked acts and thoughts.**

If, for example, he will prayerfully meditate through — or better still, if you walk with him through — Isaiah 53 and Psalm 22, *asking God to help him comprehend the breadth and depth of the Savior's suffering in his place...already having received God's full wrath as our substitute,* then he will see *how fully his sins have been covered.* And hopefully he will realize that *only pride could persuade any of us that we could do more, or add anything to Jesus' suffering and death to make us more worthy of forgiveness than His atonement has already accomplished.*

On behalf of your warrior friend, consider a couple of questions that he may be secretly asking in his wounded soul, and God's own wonderful reply from Isaiah 53.

Do you feel so __ashamed__ that you can't lift your eyes to meet the gaze of "normal" people?

Isaiah 53:3-4 assures you that He took your shame on Himself so you could be free of it.

"He was despised and forsaken of men, a man of sorrows and acquainted with grief; and like one from whom men hide their face he was despised, and we

*did not esteem Him. Surely our griefs He Himself
bore, and our sorrows He carried; yet we ourselves
esteemed Him stricken, smitten of God, and afflicted."*

We...the very wretches for whom the punishment was
due...**we** said, "God is judging Him!" The message in this
passage is that *He took your rejection and public judgment
on Himself so that you could lift up your eyes.*

We can assure him that, "there's no further need to hate
and shame yourself. Jesus took your shame to the cross. *You
can't be any more forgiven than you are."*

Even if other sinful men should believe, *as they did of
Jesus*, that you are "being punished by God," if you have
returned to Him with your guilt and shame, *you are clean*
before the only One in the universe whose judgment is *always
true and always final.* Forgiven warrior, lift your eyes!

*Do you feel that what you've done or allowed in war is so
desperately wicked you wish someone could somehow whip
the ugliness out of you, or smash you or stab you to death
and put you out of your guilty, self-condemning misery?*

*For you, Jesus already took upon Himself all the punish-
ments that you can imagine in your self-condemning soul,
so that you could once again taste joy, feel the pleasure of
friendships and family, wake up in the morning and feel the
positive anticipation of a new day.*

"He was *pierced through* for (your) transgressions, He
was *crushed* for (your) iniquities; the *chastening* for (your)

well-being fell upon Him, and by His *scourging* (*you*) are healed."

Can you punish yourself more severely, more completely, more meaningfully than the punishment He took for your sins? Listen again to this truth: if you have run to Him with your guilty wickedness you are clean before the only One in the universe whose judgment is *always true and always final.* Do not despise the forgiveness Jesus bought for you through being crushed and beaten for your guilt. Rather, receive it and embrace its peace.

New Testament scriptures as well, reveal the *sufficiency of Jesus' sacrifice and righteousness.* There are too many to list here, but they are well enough known to us. Just a few examples are:

Hebrews 10:19-23 — This wonderful passage speaks to every frightening concern: confidence to enter the holy presence of God, the sacrifice of a real, fleshly body, intercession by a perfect high priest, sincerity of heart in approaching Him, the cleansing of both conscience and body, the *foundation* of the promise of forgiveness, which is *the faithfulness of God.*

Matthew 18:21-35 — Here the emphasis is on Jesus' *requirement* that *His followers keep on forgiving* **because He forgives absolutely, and** *never quits forgiving.*

1 John 1 — Here it would help most to emphasize *God's justice* in forgiveness. Doubt always springs from the awareness of our unworthiness. How could I just say, "Sorry," and God simply says, "Okay, you're good to go"?

Warriors sense in their soul the truth of **Jeremiah 11:20,** that the "...LORD of hosts (heavenly armies) *judges righteously*...(He) tries (judges) the *feelings* and the *heart*..."

The warrior who deeply feels his uncleanness needs to know that his forgiveness is *justly* covered in Christ Jesus.

Chaplain Mike Hoyt shares the thoughts below:

> ...*fascinating and wonderful considerations. I think the last one is a key to soldier forgiveness. Soldiers believe in justice, even more than forgiveness. Some "find" forgiveness or a personal version of reconciliation through their concepts of justice. Of course, America is just and all the bad guys are unjust and had it coming. As we know justice is more about a scale of punishment than forgiveness. However, soldiers cannot accept the idea of forgiveness without spending a lot of time understanding how justice (their own accountability to right and wrong) can work simultaneously in a Holy God who forgives. We have to demonstrate God's just way to deal with life even as He also "justly" forgives. For soldiers, forgiveness cannot occur without justice. The shadows of guilt, shame, injustice are specters of a "just war" and have to be somehow addressed in the Truth of Christ as the propitiation (satisfier of justice) as well as the Savior of broken souls.* Romans 3:26; 1 Peter 3:18; 2 Corinthians 5:21; 1 John 4:10

SPIRITUALITY

This term is important — not because it is uniquely related to combat and to the warrior's soul, any more than the previous three terms discussed — but because it is *more urgently related to the life-or-death outcome of war for the combatant,* than to those of us who don't consciously and knowingly face death each day.

Societies are made up of sinful men incessantly looking for ways to make life work without submitting to the authority, wisdom, and guidance of the One Who designed and created us. People everywhere are always experimenting with philosophies and self-made religions they hope will solve the *"problem" of God* and *His claim to authority over our lives and eternal destiny.*

At various times, fresh versions of the philosophy of *materialism* have cropped up. It grew so strong in American educational institutions in the '60s and '70s that the question of any "spiritual" dimension of life was laughed out of the classroom, and "religion" was concluded to be useless mythology.

In recent years, however, this deadly philosophy has been challenged by the undeniable realization dawning on people, including many philosophers and scientists, that we are more than biomachines, that there *is in fact* a "spiritual dimension" to us.

In whatever way this spiritual reality may be viewed, our current society, including military society, is compelled to acknowledge its existence. In fact, as already noted, for the military today *spiritual health* is depicted as one of the pillars of *resilience — which is the capability of continuing in, or getting back into, the fight.* Resilience is the goal; and *"spirituality"* is one of the tools that are useful to that end.

The therapist's project from the official perspective is to help the warrior discover his own version of spirituality and tap into whatever strength it may offer to increase his resilience. This may involve any number of options, such as reengaging with his own religious background, getting in touch with the god within him, looking to some higher power, or, to put it plainly, whatever works for him "spiritually."

With this realization has come opportunity for believing caregivers to clearly explain spiritual truth to our warriors in the crucial context of life, death, and eternity. We must articulate the truth that Jeremiah repeatedly drives home in the 11th chapter of his prophecy, that unclear or misplaced "spirituality" is not helpful, but rather supremely *dangerous.* Jeremiah says that what is absolutely essential is to *hear* and *heed* the *words* of God. If we neglect or refuse to hear **the words of God with which He reveals Himself and His will,** Jeremiah says we bring spiritual disaster upon ourselves. This is not a random search for some useful "spirituality."

Young warriors don't usually pause to contemplate these philosophical-sounding questions until they're being medevaced with life-threatening injuries, or are facing desperately difficult post-traumatic issues, including severe feelings of guilt.

In fact, statistical studies of the pool of "emerging adults" from which these young warriors extract themselves to voluntarily fight our battles for us, reveal that the "spiritual rug" has been almost completely pulled from under them by our culture, educational institutions, and many biblically depleted churches before they ever reach the battlefield and face eternal issues in the living color of blood.

In their book, *Souls In Transition, The Religious And Spiritual Lives Of Emerging Adults,* authors Christian Smith and Patricia Snell give some summaries, in a variety of categories, of the *"religious" state of these young "emerging adults."* This is the state *in which they arrive for training to become combatants.*

Below are a few observations I've drawn from their study that reveal the **beliefs young warriors bring with them to engage the ultimate enemy, death:**

57 percent of emerging adults believe that *many religions may be true.*

40 percent of "conservative Protestants" (read, "evangelicals,") agree that it is okay to pick and choose religious beliefs.

Most emerging adults say the core principles of all "important" religions are the same. So people can choose different faiths for themselves, and *anybody who follows any particular religion is ultimately just like any other religious person following any other religion.*

It is their subjective personal sense of what *seems right to them*...what fits their experience...what makes sense to them given their viewpoint...*that decides for emerging adults what to believe or practice in religion.*

They believe that *the purpose of religion is to support individuals.* In this sense they don't mind having a conversation on the "topic" of spirituality or religion but, personally, they are indifferent to it. What really motivates and informs their lives is *their own feelings and inclinations.*

They believe that they can *subjectively determine* what is right, worthy and important. However, paradoxically, the study reveals that they are *doubtful* of their own personal conclusions...even *sometimes paralyzed by awareness of the relativity of their personal perspective.* At bottom they believe that ultimately *nobody can really know what is true or right.* In fact, they've been taught that *real knowledge and final truth are illusions.*

*Therefore—they are persuaded that **all knowledge and value claims are really arbitrary exertions of power and control over the other person.***

This final point helps explain the extreme applications of "pluralism" that our culture has adopted. *In short, then, to choose one form of religion or spirituality over another is your right. But to seek to persuade someone else of it is simply your effort to exert your own arbitrary power and control over him.* As we've already seen, *God's version of "pluralism"* is found in a nutshell in Jeremiah Chapter 11.

The point in all this is the need *to address the understanding of spirituality the warrior takes with him into battle, where the "feelings and inclinations" he's been following may instantly determine his eternal destiny.*

What is he to think?

As if to specifically illustrate this point, two days ago I received the following message from a co-worker regarding an infantry soldier:

> *"I just met (this soldier's) wife at chapel today and she is desperate that her husband...come to know Christ. They have two boys–about 5 and 10–who attend chapel with her...(her husband) questions the authority and claims of Scripture, given the multitude of choices on the menu..."*

In the present conflict with radical Muslim groups in the war against terrorism, there is increasingly a further complication of this question of spirituality for the warrior.

What is he to think of the "spiritual" questions that arise from his new face-to-face awareness that the people he is in mortal combat with on behalf of his "Christian" nation may be far more religious in the practice of their version of spirituality than is he?

This is __not__ a "hypothetical question."

It's an unpleasant circumstance to speak of that, when not on duty, or between operations, a significant number of our young warriors may be gathered around their laptops watching pornography while in nearby quarters their host nation military counterparts may be attentively preparing themselves for prayers (of course, between prayers, many of them will be using the same pornography.)

*The point is that our warrior **has now come to know this of himself and of the others***; *and this conflicting sense of "spirituality" complicates the damage done to his soul by combat, and muddies the meaning and process of post-traumatic spiritual recovery.*

Consider the perspective he brings with him as he approaches war:

- He has been taught an amorphous pick-and-choose spirituality;
- "Moderate" Islam has been growing fast in his own country;

- The therapeutic counsel he is receiving assures him that one god or religion is as "true" as another.

How is he to be sure that he himself is not the moral offender in the war?

More than one combatant has raised this question with me.

I don't have statistics for this, but from my personal conversations with our combatants, and from extensive reading of materials emerging from the battle space, I'm quite sure that many of our young warriors *perceive themselves* as daily facing — not "terrorists" — but young combatants like themselves, fighting for their families and religious values.

Except for the moments when they are actually shooting at him (or obviously brutalizing their own people,) he takes it "on faith" that they are the "bad guys."

If we care for the *soul* of the warrior, *we must help him find God-breathed answers to these questions*. To reinforce the *necessity of biblically based counsel* by godly chaplains, pastors, and others who care for the souls of combatants, I'll repeat a paraphrased statement from a VA counseling resource which may be the main guidance he has thus far received.

Spirituality is that which gives a person meaning and purpose. It is found in relationships with self, others, ideas, nature, and possibly a higher power...spiritual distress arises when one of these relationships that provide meaning is threatened or broken. The more significant a particular relationship is, the greater the severity of spiritual distress...

Spiritual wholeness is restored when that which threatens or breaks...is removed, transformed, integrated, or transcended.

Therefore, the warrior is further counseled that *a potential positive outcome of post-combat trauma is that rather than accepting standard moral systems that might not support actions in war, veterans can develop a more mature, moral way of living. The unique self develops its own way of living morally in the world.*

At this point I will ask another challenging question for the sake of caregivers who believe that God's Word is truth. Again, *this is **not** a hypothetical question.* We have seen its answer worked out in terrorist acts conducted by our own citizens and military members who decided on *another* form of "spirituality."

What if a young warrior experiencing "spiritual distress" decides that the "more mature moral way of living for his unique self" means embracing the most radical teachings of Islam?

Just like the rest of us, warriors treasure the sense that spirituality is their "link" to God and moral accountability, not merely their relationship to "something significant."(Romans 1) This is demonstrated in my earlier quotes from the men themselves, and in earlier quotes under Chronic Spiritual Conflict In Warriors.

It's painful to contemplate that *a nation with Christian heritage would send its young people into mortal combat with official endorsement of the importance of spirituality, and yet allow it to remain for them such a nebulous and confusing concept.* Our national commitment to official pluralism does not allow for any particular definition or expression of spirituality to be elevated above, or articulated at the expense of, any other.

*Therefore, in keeping with our national posture, **official military doctrine can sincerely assure the warrior of the importance of spirituality, but cannot narrow the definition of it to the point where he may decide to embrace a true relationship with Jesus Christ*** that will give him eternal hope, guide him with reliable truth as he faces the moral issues of war, and see him through the spiritual darkness of combat.

This remains the responsibility of those who care not solely for the physical and emotional resilience of the warrior, *but for the state of his soul before God.* We must appropriately, courageously, and confidently guide him into a true understanding of God's message of sin, righteousness, judgment, redemption, and eternal confidence, through faith in the one true Savior.

13.

THE PROBLEM OF THE WARRIOR'S EARLY-FORMED MISUNDERSTANDINGS AND CONFUSION ABOUT GOD

Considering then, as we've said, that many warriors have *early-formed and long-held misunderstandings and confused thoughts of God*, the question that confronts them is, **who is qualified** to **speak for God**, *to correct or clarify these impressions, and set him free from fear and doubt?* The answer of course is this: it is *only those who are able to provide clear understanding drawn directly from the written Word of God.*

Let me bring to life some of these early-formed misunderstandings about God, judgment, and grace by sharing a few comments I've personally heard from warriors:

"There's no point in my getting saved now. I'm just going to go out and kill people."

"Killing got to be a rush. We went looking for people to kill. When we were told to take prisoners, we didn't. We killed them anyway." This was spoken in a spirit of hopeless remorse by a young Marine who has not known how to "face" God since that time.

"A .50 cal round had taken out most of her pelvis...I don't know why she was still alive, and I was 19 then so there was a lot I didn't know. I couldn't help her so I gave her a lethal dose of morphine." This medic was dealing with the question, "Was it mercy or presumption in God's sight?"

"The city was under curfew. The rules of engagement were: 'anyone on the street is an enemy combatant.' We found a group of men and women in an alley. Some were armed with AKs. My corporal was screaming at me, 'Shoot them! Shoot them!' And finally I did. But I've never pulled the trigger since, unless someone was shooting at me." This young warrior's heart was sick with remorse as he told me the story, even though he had followed orders in accord with the Rules Of Engagement.

Following are some examples of combat-induced spiritual conflict that is rooted in a lack of true or adequate understanding of God.

In, *The Forever War,* Dexter Filkins tells of a conversation he had with a young Christian corporal during a lull in the fighting. The soldier talks about the church he came from back home. *He was raised to think killing was bad...something people do in gangs.* In training he had wondered what it would be like to kill somebody, and wasn't sure he could.

Now he has "shot a couple of guys," and he says *"he isn't sure if he feels that much."* The best he's been able to figure is that when they attack, you shoot, and you get to go home to your family. Otherwise they kill you and then they go on killing everybody else. *He will bring this sad perplexity about killing home in his soul for his pastor or church leaders to help him sort out.* Are they ready?

In, *The Only Thing Worth Dying For*, Eric Blehm tells of the evening prayer of a Special Forces Soldier in combat. The soldier asks God to forgive him if he was sinning by having too much fun today pulling the trigger. In his prayer he recalls how the Lord had spared his life in a previous deployment and how he had failed to "walk God's path" when he got home. This time, he tells the Lord, "I ain't making no promises." All he asks now of God is that if anything happens to him, God will take care of his family and let them know he loves them.

He finishes his prayer with these words, *"Forgive me my sins. I accept you as my Lord and Savior. Amen."*

It is for good reason that we labor to help the warrior know and understand God. Within days this S.F. soldier was delivered by "friendly fire" into the presence of God.

In *Ambush Alley: The Most Extraordinary Battle Of The Iraq War,* author Tim Pritchard tells how a *death in the unit has ignited in one warrior a confused internal argument about the very existence of God.* Now the soldier is engaged in an *inner battle* that he knows will come to its climax in eternity. The force he's up against in this battle is the question: how could a *good* God have let his buddy be killed? His struggle then brings him to reluctantly allow that it was *God, in His goodness, Who saved him.* The battle only intensifies however. His early-formed misunderstanding of God has led him to yield to the possibility that there *may actually be* a God, *but it has not led him to a place of peace.* Rather, he has arrived at an *even greater distress*, because *"...if there is a God then I'm really...because I've been out there killing people."*

In *House To House, An Epic Memoir of War*, John Bruning gives us another penetrating account of a warrior's *spiritual confusion* in the midst of *physical combat.* This soldier, the recipient of the Silver Star for heroism, is a professing Christian.

The account starts with this strong young soldier aloofly watching from a distance while his battalion chaplain prays with a group of soldiers as they prepare to launch an operation. But he finds himself unable to remain detached, and the scenario he's observing sets him *"...thinking about my own faith, or what's left of it."* (A Marine SGT friend, reading these words in my manuscript, expressed aching identification with them.)

This battle-proven warrior has come from a strong Christian home where he had, himself, been very spiritually active. But *he declares that his time in Iraq has convinced him that God doesn't want to hear from him any more. He has reached the conclusion that **he has become a killer**.* He wants to kill... yearns to kill his enemies. *But the conflict in his soul is only* *inflamed by this confession.* He tries to reassure himself that he believes in God and there is *"a reverence for the Almighty that lies deep inside me."*

In his conflicted sadness he resigns himself to the awareness that **when he returns home he will be an alien. This realization leaves him feeling utterly alone, and cold with fear.** (Again, my Marine SGT friend tells me he deeply identifies with this feeling.)

For our own growth as caregivers, we need to consider this scenario: suppose this young man came home from war longing for resolution of the conflict in his soul and restoration to peace with God...*and God presented him to you or me.*

Who is qualified to speak for God? Are we prepared to receive him into our hearts along with all his war-induced confusion and the emotional alienation that's etched into his soul? And will we have *relevant understanding of truth from God that his soul needs?*

14.

WHAT *PRACTICAL* STEPS CAN WE TAKE TO HELP THE WARRIOR OVERCOME HIS SOUL CONFLICT?

In these observations about the tenacious soul conflict our warriors experience, so far I've said little about *how* to "make contact" and become a friend worthy of his opening his heart to our care. What I'll share here is an experience-based but admittedly inadequate starting point...an expression of my own effort to grow in understanding of how to breach the barriers of pain and confusion and help our warriors overcome the *soul conflict* that results from "committing" war. I'm constantly learning more as I minister to, and interact with, combat-impacted officers, enlisted infantrymen, chaplains, medics and others whose souls have been brutalized by war.

It's apparent from the quotes and comments I've inserted that, as I record lessons learned, I'm also sharing these written thoughts with the warriors themselves, and with other caregivers for their adjustments, clarifications, insights, observations, and affirmations. I'm also hoping to continue learning from fellow servants who minister to warriors out of the unfailing truth of God's Word. So as you read these words, please feel free to contact me and share your own wisdom and insight.

We must pray and labor to understand the answers to these simple, honest questions:

- **How can I find my way into the heart of the warrior to help him?**
- **Where do I start?**
- **What do I begin to say that won't bring down the curtain?**
- **If he does begin to open up, and reveals something disappointing, shocking or even horrific that I'm not emotionally or spiritually prepared for, what do I do or say next?**

Honestly, I'm not very good at systematizing questions and answers...in fact, I tend to be repelled by the process because it so often produces "systematic approaches" by people trying to "do" ministry. Broken, conflicted hearts are not served well by "checklist" questions and answers, and I don't believe there is a "one-size-fits-all" approach. Every soul-traumatized warrior is unique in his or her history, war experience, fears, and much more. Every one has to be loved, listened to, and known first as a unique human being *whose soul has been subjected to the* **moral chaos** *of war.*

The following comment by my Infantry MAJ friend gives us some in-stride encouragement and guidance as we continue to learn and grow.

> *"... remind them that although dealing with PTSD requires some education and awareness it is still incarnational, discipleship ministry at its core. By sharing your life you gain the right to be heard.* (I'll insert here that the real beginning is gaining the privilege of *hearing.*) *By listening, praying and being guided by the Holy Spirit you can discern the true spiritual issues. Through confession the warrior can receive forgiveness. Through the application of wisdom and the Word of God the warrior can gain healing. Through sound Bible teaching and discussion their inaccurate views of God can be corrected."*

FOUNDATIONAL SUGGESTIONS

Here are some basic thoughts that may be helpful in approaching a warrior suffering the *soul damage* that results from the moral chaos of war.

- *First, take the initiative* in pursuing the communication and take the time to show yourself a trustworthy friend and a humble servant, willing to listen to his story *(from as far back as his childhood),* or to support him in prayer for as much as he's willing to share. It's true; our efforts at pursuing the contact may or may not be welcomed. But if we allow ourselves to remain so "safely" busy with routine ministry that we *never try to reach them*, then the warriors are unlikely to reach out to us. The familiar questions apply: "If not I, who? If not now, when?"

• *No demands or expectations...*one of the most important lessons I've learned is to humbly recognize that *he doesn't owe me anything...*not his time, not his attention, not his respect, not a response. I'll serve him if he will allow it. And, before God, it's my responsibility to try.

Earlier, I mentioned the ministry of *The Anchor,* a downtown servicemen's center in Oceanside, CA near Camp Pendleton. During the more than four years my wife and I served there, our greatest number of contacts were with new Marines while they were in the School Of Infantry (Advanced Infantry Training,) and Navy Corpsmen in Field Medical Services School...and then, increasingly, to those returning from combat deployments.

Although by the time we came to *The Anchor* we had already been serving God among the various branches of the military for thirty-five years, it would take another book to describe all the ministry lessons I learned in that period of time. But this one...*no demands or expectations*... is one of those that came through loud and clear.

When we assumed leadership of the ministry we also assumed responsibility for leading and training the volunteers who assisted in the kitchen and those who helped with the welcoming and "counseling" ministry. The folks who helped with evangelism and counseling were a blessing to work with, and they loved the young Marines. However, some who were former military themselves instinctively adopted an authoritative style of communication, in some cases even to the extent of being unwilling to let a Marine leave the place without having made a profession of faith and signing a slip of paper to attest to it.

The Marines at this stage of their training were in such a state of general intimidation that they would virtually sit at attention in front of the plate of food we'd provided until the counselor was finished with them. Then they'd often give the expected response, eat, and exit the place...sometimes joking with their buddies about the experience as they walked out. I was immediately reminded of the saying I'd heard long ago from a teacher: *"A man convinced against his will is of the same opinion still."* This lesson helped us exercise greater wisdom in training our volunteers.

The experience I've just described was with men involved in intense training *in **preparation** for combat.*

Ministry to warriors **returning** *from combat* was equally educational.

In the first place, they were less likely to come into the center; and when they did come in, they were no longer willing to sit still and listen to a mini-sermon just for a lunch. Their hearts and their countenances were harder. If we couldn't find a way of connecting with them at a deeper, more personal level, they wouldn't hesitate to walk out.

I realized that *God was putting me through a more advanced school of love...learning to more deeply and genuinely love these young warriors who had by now tasted a new and intense form of "brother love" through combat.* They were teaching me that genuinely probing their lives and their war-influenced hearts must be done in a spirit of humility and respect. This meant being willing to ask questions that might initially be ignorant and out of touch...*but not careless or presumptuous.* And it meant persevering in our care for them until they began to open their hearts. *In other words, they began to teach me how to love warriors.*

I learned even more deeply the lesson that they didn't owe me anything...what was a sandwich or bowl of soup, chips, cake, and a soft drink compared to what they had now given of themselves in combat? On the other hand, I was more aware than ever of how much *I owed them: first*, gratitude, and then a clear, humble, *relevant* presentation of the gospel. I became keenly aware that I was enjoying the privilege of speaking to them because they had come home alive...this time.

• *Find ways* **to give him your undivided attention,** *away from the general group* in your ministry. This is fundamentally important. For the many reasons already discussed, *the warrior will not likely take the risk of asking you for your personal attention*; and he certainly won't want to make it a public thing.

• *If he'll agree to meet with you, ask him to choose a place where he'll be comfortable*...coffee shop, restaurant, long walk outdoors, or anything he feels good about. Stay away from traffic and crowds unless he chooses such a place. If you meet at a place indoors, I recommend that it *not* be an "office." Make sure there's space for privacy. Make the place comfortable, and let him choose where to sit — without making a drama of it.

*When it's possible, I enjoy (actually prefer) taking long walks with the friends I'm caring for...*especially alongside some beautiful lake or stream, or some other pleasant, soothing surroundings. This way you may spend two or three private, calming, releasing hours together, hardly realizing the time has passed. In my experience, this can be more fruitful than sitting together, almost anywhere, for an hour a week.

- **When you meet up with him, or at any other time, don't approach him from behind and surprise him.** Especially don't lay hands on him from behind.

  This is *not* to say that physical contact — a hand on the shoulder or some other warm human contact — is inappropriate. At the right time, it's an important part of the healing process. Just don't startle or surprise him if you can avoid it. This "startle" issue may be more important to some warriors than to others, depending on the circumstances that created his trauma. But it's a good thing to avoid in any case.

- **Unless he plunges right into what's on his heart, which he probably won't do, you might begin by just asking him to tell you what's occupying his mind since he returned home.** Or perhaps, what has given him the most pleasure about being home. This may surprise you by triggering negative thoughts, rather than positive; but that's the beginning of communication.

• *Listen with your heart and all your attention to what he's trying to convey* (but relax, don't sit on the edge of your seat and stare at him.) What he *begins* to allow you to hear will be only the safe elements of his story, and the tip of the emotional and spiritual iceberg. Don't criticize, judge or correct what he shares. And don't be quick to draw conclusions. *This truly is the beginning of a marathon, not a sprint. This can be really challenging, because of our strong desire to help him, and our habitual tendency to tell information we've learned in the past.*

• *Don't try to talk back or begin to "fix" him with familiar teachings or Bible texts.* You don't yet have any real idea of the story behind what he begins to share, so how can you *meaningfully* apply the Words of God at this point? Listen, listen, listen, and learn. When you ask questions, let the purpose be to know his heart more deeply and meaningfully, not to ferret out "useful" information.

• *As he begins to open his heart, what he needs to hear or sense is: "I'm listening, I'll (really) pray for you and support you in what you share with me, and I want to hear more when you're ready to talk again."*

If you respond at all at this point, let it be *plain*, *honest*, *sympathetic* responses to what you're hearing. Here's an example of a heart-felt, well-meaning effort of mine that *missed* the man's heart.

My friend, a big, strong Marine with "Christian" background and a huge smile, became very close to us in our ministry at The Anchor. Before his first combat deployment, he used to accompany us to the churches near the base as we represented the center ministry. His presence was a pleasure.

During his first deployment to Iraq his platoon was engaged in incessant vicious fighting in Najaf, Fallujah, and Ramadi. Some of his friends died, and he nearly did. When he returned to Pendleton after his deployment, he came out to the center to see us. As he walked in the door I was stunned. His smile was a grimace, and he was obviously not seeing us through the same eyes. He told me ugly, painful stories of fighting, and of his abandonment to it.

He also told me of a post-deployment event in San Diego, when a foolish civilian had approached him and his friends and made a derogatory comment about them and the war. My friend instantly hit the man in the face with the heel of his hand, knocking him to the ground.

Hearing this, I was suddenly afraid for him and exclaimed, "Oh, you've given so much already! Don't risk spending years in prison!" I was feeling so protective of him; I didn't understand how my comment missed his heart.

After his second combat deployment in Iraq, we rarely saw him any more. He still loved us and treated us almost as second parents...he just didn't come around any more. If I could go back to that moment when he told me about the incident in San Diego, my reaction would be very different.

*At the time, honestly, I had <u>two</u> strong feelings, but I've only mentioned one of them...**fear** on his behalf. My other feeling was empathetic **anger** against the mindless civilian who had verbally assaulted him. Now, if I found myself in that same moment with him, my exclamation would be, "If you hadn't hit that guy, I would have!"*

Of course I wouldn't have done that...nor would he have wanted me to. But it is, in fact, how I felt. And that honest comment would have helped him see that I "got" his pain and anger. He didn't need my "protection." He needed someone to "hear" him — to understand the validity of his anger. Only the Lord

243

knows, but maybe it would have made a difference in my future opportunity to minister to him.

• *During the course of your meetings with your soul-damaged friend ask God to grant understanding or spiritual insight into the key elements of his soul pain or conflict and how they relate to revealed truth about God.* You may spend hours in fellowship with him before you begin to apprehend relevant truth that will begin to set him free.

• *Don't scout for a "fix."* Stay focused on listening to the heart of your friend, and helping him come to *know God* in the context of his struggles. In due time, *God will show you both* the healing truth he can identify with and respond to.

• *Don't expect one discovery or insight to "cure" his problems overnight. Awareness is only the beginning.* This is where your physical walk with him takes on the spiritual dimension of walking with him through the questions, doubts, and setbacks that follow. You'll need to help him discover the steps he needs to take to begin to reject the enemy's lies against him, and to embrace forgiveness and grace.

• *Pay attention when he reports small setbacks or victories.* Take time to *consider* how they relate to the big picture *of his struggle and help him tie the pieces together in his understanding* of God's grace and forgiveness.

- **As his soul begins to show signs of restoration, talk with him about the restoration of his "body."** Help him see the *meaning* of any emotional and physiological events in relationship to the healing of his soul conflict. As his soul is being set free, his body will begin to respond.
I want to re-emphasize that we are speaking specifically of *soul damage* here, and of the restoration of the *"outer man"* that is directly related to it.

There are emotional/psychological residues of combat affecting the physical body, such as the stresses of hyper-vigilance, and the re-experiencing of traumatic events, that are not specifically causing spiritual conflict, and may be helped by various counseling approaches. In speaking of the restoration of the warrior's *"body"* through the healing of his soul, I'm referring to the *body's expressions* of the conflict in the soul.
But remember that emotional-psychological symptoms help us find the path to the soul issues, and may in fact be directly related to the soul's conflict.

- **As he gains spiritual strength and his outer man begins to heal (freedom from spiritual fear, guilt, hatred, etc.), then through prayer and conversation, we can begin to** *help him take some steps in opening himself to restored* <u>*relational*</u> *connections...letting down the wall of isolation.* This process may lead him through complications such as feeling vulnerable, angry reactions, disdain for trivial non-combatant activities, or disappointments. He will probably need help in just finding *value* in social relationships with civilians, and in tolerating people's ignorance of what he has been required to experience to preserve for them their self-indulgent lifestyles.

• *Try to discover and/or design some form of community reintegration ceremony for your warriors.*
An email conversation I had with a co-worker was thought-provoking. It went like this:

To me:
"Have you given any meditation and thought to the Purification Ceremony in **Numbers 31:19-24?** A chaplain brought this passage to my attention and thinks our culture doesn't have a way to integrate warriors back into civilian life. It seems like the chaplains should be on the forefront of this. "

My reply:
I agree with your chaplain friend that our culture doesn't have a comprehensive and coherent way to integrate warriors back into civilian life, although there are efforts being made in some Christian communities and churches. In general, it

doesn't seem that the *purposeful restoration and reintegration* of our warriors is on most civilian churches' radar. In fact I don't think we have a coherent means for this in the body of Christ.

I also agree with you in that *one would think* chaplains would be on the cutting edge of this concern. However, as I'm sure you have seen, the chaplains themselves are often the ones in need of caring support and reintegration. A Division chaplain at an Army Infantry Post I served was so burdened about 'helping the helpers' that he compiled a list of trustworthy folks to whom he could refer his chaplains when they returned from deployment and he included me in the list. His message to his young chaplains was, "choose who you want to talk to, but you must talk to someone."

I observed that the chaplains did pretty much the same as the infantrymen...quietly ignored the order. For their own unique and honorable reasons, many chaplains, like the grunts they serve, feel they *shouldn't need* to be helped. And yet they themselves may, in fact, be feeling overwhelmed.

When chaplains return home they face all the same re-entry and family pressures the warriors do, plus the pastoral care of the returned combatants and their families, and much more. Not much time and emotional energy remain to explore creative avenues for troop reintegration...and that's only speaking of the military community, which is yet a far cry from trying to reach out to the widely varied churches in the civilian community and help them build a cohesive reentry plan.

The Numbers 31 passage doesn't seem to me a salient help in our situation. It refers to ceremonial purification of anyone who has been in touch with a dead body, not only of combatants. It's not really a cultural "welcome home," but a ceremonial *self*-purification that is tied to the Levitical system.

Your comments did set my mind on a path that might be helpful to us in the ministry community or the chapel communities where we fellowship.

My thoughts went first to a re-integration ceremony that my Intel Col friend talked about in his Veterans Day message. In my earlier reference, I only included his words about wanting forgiveness. But take a look at these words from the same message:

"We mean well but sometimes, no one explained how to bring these warriors back into our church, our communities or our families.A Chaplain friend of mine explained that he thought the American Indians did it best. They do two ceremonies when a soldier returns.

The first is they light a "healing fire" and then the youngest woman in the tribe uses the ashes to mark the forehead and cheeks of everyone in the tribe. Then, for the soldier, a woman in the tribe, usually the mother cleans the ashes away and explains that this is washing away the tears, the fears and cleansing everyone in the tribe of the horrible experiences from the war. Then the oldest woman in the tribe dries the soldier's face.

In the other ceremony the oldest woman in the tribe paints the hands of the soldier red, another woman, usually the mother, washes them. Then the youngest woman or the fiancé or wife of the soldier, dries them. I am not advocating that we hold this kind of a ceremony. I was just explaining what it may be like for a few."

My friend, the 75th Ranger Regimental chaplain, shared the following story with me of a ceremony he, while a Ranger Battalion chaplain, had conducted for his men before they left the battle space. His goal was to help them begin their reintegration process while still in the war zone.

"Before my deployment to Iraq I was spending time thinking about the challenges our warriors go through especially as it related to killing of other human beings. I was reading through Numbers and in chapter 31 I was struck by the declaration that those who had killed others or touched the dead were unclean and the command to purify themselves prior to returning to the camp. My reaction was one of anger. God was the one who had called these men to do battle and to kill other human beings and now he declares them unclean. I know it was part of the entire

Law, which was much bigger than this particular battle, but it still struck me as unjust. Upon further prayer and thinking about the situation it dawned upon me that these ancient warriors were the same as ours. They had participated in a terrible battle and even those that may not have killed were still knee deep in blood and guts (I can attest that being in this situation can really inspire a need for cleansing). This ceremonial uncleanness and ritual purification is never for God. It is for us.

"In this particular situation it was about a group of warriors being able to enter their society with their heads held high, knowing that their souls were good before both God and the community of faith. Their souls were deeply affected by this warfare and they needed tangible reminders of the intangible. Our need for these reminders and mileposts has not changed. The ancient Jews had the tabernacle/temple and the rituals that pointed to the living God. We as Christians have the Lord's Supper to remind us of all that Jesus sacrificed for us.

"I decided to think of tangible ways that I could help warriors reintegrate into a society that knows very little of what they have done and endured. Upon redeployment from a 15-month deployment to Iraq, where

we spilled a lot of blood, I executed a purification ceremony for my battalion. Right before boarding planes to leave Iraq we gathered around a huge bonfire with torches. I had a drummer playing different beats to match each part of the ceremony. I started by letting the commander tell them that they had done all their country had called them to do and more. They had made a difference. I took over and talked about how they had suffered while they were here and we had lost some of our brothers in the course of 15 months. As I read the name of each of our fallen, one of their friends brought a large stone to stack in front of the fire. After that, I had instructed every person to grab a small stone and lay it on top of the others. I paraphrased from Joshua and how he had the elders stack stones so that everyone would always remember what The Lord had done. I told them that they should hold their memories close and that they can serve as a personal memorial so that we can look back at all that has happened in proper perspective.

"I then spoke about how not only had our blood been shed but we had shed much blood. The vast majority was from those who were fighting us but some because of tragic accidents. I explained how the blood stains us but it can be washed away. It was a mandatory ceremony so I was trying to be very cautious in the

Christian content of the message. I told them that this cleansing was not for the forgiveness of anything. But the message is that there were some things that could and should stay in Iraq and they should be able to reenter society with nothing to be ashamed of in this regard. I was worried that my message may not be received in the right way but I think it hit home because immediately after the ceremony three soldiers who I had been working with came to me and declared their intention to be baptized."

I recently read of a homecoming event that took place at the close of WWII as the U.S. Naval fleet returned home to New York harbor. This element of their return wasn't exactly a community-provided "welcome home," but rather, the fleet sailors created an amazing homecoming event for themselves and their home community.

On their arrival in port, the ships welcomed aboard 1,000 needy children. Someone had orchestrated the collection of the children's clothing measurements before the ships reached port, and these disadvantaged children were brought aboard and presented perfectly fitted navy-blue coats and woolen caps, all gift-wrapped and waiting for them. These vessels of war had been transformed into carriers of compassion to their homeport. If *being valued* plays a significant part in the warrior's sense of being loved and welcomed home, then surely these sailors played a vital role on their own behalf in the reintegration process.

I wonder whether returning warriors today could, with the initiation and guidance of their battalion chaplains and other spiritual leaders in their units, create some similar concepts that would help build bridges of their own making to their home communities. The exercise itself would surely help restart the important *sense of belonging*, and by it's outgoing nature perhaps even begin to open some doors of communication with "normal" folks.

I hope that, from examples like these from warrior leaders, we can draw wisdom and practical ideas with which to welcome our warrior-ambassadors back into our lives and communities.

With prayerful creativity, in our various ministry communities we can undoubtedly devise ceremonies that:

1. Meaningfully value the warrior for his sacrificial service,
2. Show understanding of the inexpressible things he's been required to see and do, without having to name the specifics,
3. Acknowledge the hard road of healing he faces,
4. Celebrate his presence with us.

I have quoted an AF Special Operator who made it clear that *feeling valued was what helped him most in re-integration*. The hard part of this is that most people, *even in the military community, don't know* and understand deeply *what* our warriors experience. For such ceremonies to be developed there will have to be some training and guidance. I believe that with godly cooperation and good guidance from established warriors, we can create such welcome home events. And this may also form a foundation for the warrior to *feel safe in reaching out for ongoing help.*

I hope these closing thoughts may serve as a starting line in our efforts to find our way into the damaged hearts of our warrior friends, where we may walk with them out of the darkness and into the sunlight from on high.

Additionally, I hope there has been stirred among fellow soul caregivers a desire for further conversation and helpful interaction. I welcome further guidance and instruction for myself from fellow servants of our warriors, as well as from warriors themselves who read this.

SELECTED REFERENCES

Dean, Chuck. *Nam Vet, Making Peace With Your Past.* Charles A. Dean, 1987

Cantrell, Bridget C., Ph.D., and Chuck Dean. *Once A Warrior, Wired For Life.* WordSmith Books, LLC, 2007

Dean, Chuck, and Betty Nordberg. *When The War Is Over A New One Begins.* WordSmith Books, LLC, 2003.

Cantrell, Bridget C., Ph.D., and Chuck Dean. *Down Range to Iraq and Back.* WordSmith Books, LLC, 2005

Cantrell, Bridget C., Ph.D. *Souls Under Siege, The Effects of Multiple Troop Deployments–and How to Weather The Storm.* Hearts Toward Home International, 2009

Kay, Ellie. *Heroes At Home: Help and Hope for America's Military Families.* Bethany House Publishers, 2012

Brown, LTC Calvin. *War Zone, Hope Beyond Carnage.* Christian Services Network, 2006

Adsit, Rev. Chris. *The Combat Trauma Healing Manual.* Military Ministry Press, Campus Crusade/Cru, 2007

Smiley, Captain Scotty, with Doug Crandall. *Hope Unseen.* Howard Books/Simon & Schuster, 2010

Smith, Christian, with Patricia Snell. *Souls In Transition, The Religious & Spiritual Lives Of Emerging Adults.* Oxford University Press, 2009

Grossman, Lt. Col. (Ret.) David. Website Article http://www.recoverytoday.net/2011/55-august/350-the-myth-of-our-returning-veterans-and-violent-crime

Clark, Allen. Founder, Website: *combatfaith.com*

Croft, Dr. Harry A., M.D., with Rev. Dr. Chrys Parker, J.D. *I Always Sit With My Back To The Wall.* Stillpoint Media Services, 2011

Martin, Nathan. *"Will God Forgive?"* Website Article: OMF Publishers, OMF.org>US>Peoples and Places>Stories>Cambodia Stories> Will God Forgive?

Plekenpol, Captain Christopher. *Faith In The Fog Of War —vol. II*. In-Him Ministries, Inc., 2007

Wallace, Kathryn. *Building The Warrior Brain*. Readers Digest Article, February, 2013 issue.

Grossman, Lt. Col. (Ret.) Dave. *On Killing, The Psychological Cost of Learning To Kill in War and Society*. Back Bay Books, 1995

Mansfield, Stephen. *The Faith of The American Soldier*. Charisma House, 2005

Robinson, Linda. *Masters of Chaos, The Secret History of The Special Forces*. PublicAffairs, 2004

Hogan, J.B. *From Basic To Baghdad, A Soldier Writes Home*. Brave Ideas, 2005

Fury, Dalton. *Kill Bin Laden*. St. Martin's Griffin, 2008

Wright, Evan. *Generation Kill*. Berkley Caliber, 2004

Yon, Michael. *Moment of Truth In Iraq*. Richard Vigilante Books, 2008

Mullaney, Craig M. *The Unforgiving Minute, A Soldier's Education*. The Penguin Press, 2009

Naylor, Sean. *Not A Good Day To Die, The Untold Story of Operation Anaconda*. Berkley Caliber, 2005

North, Oliver. *American Heroes, In The Fight Against Radical Islam*. B&H Books, 2008

Burden, Matthew Currier. *The Blog Of War, Front-Line Dispatches From Soldiers In Iraq*. Simon & Schuster, 2006

Wiener, Tom. *Forever A Soldier, Unforgettable Stories of Wartime Service*. Nat. Geographic, 2005

Gilbertson, Ashley. *Whiskey Tango Foxtrot, A Photographer's Chronicle of The Iraq War*. University of Chicago Press 2007

Coll, Steve. *Ghost Wars, The Secret History of The CIA, Afghanistan and Bin Laden from the Soviet Invasion to September 10, 2001*. Penguin Books, 2004

Crews, Robert D., and Amin Tarzi. *The Taliban and The Crisis of Afghanistan*. Harvard Univ. Press, 2008

Bellavia, David, and John Bruning. *House To House, An Epic Memoir of War*. Simon & Schuster Free Press, 2007

Rashid, Ahmed. *Descent Into Chaos: The U.S. and the Disaster in Pakistan, Afghanistan, and Central Asia*. Penguin Group, 2008

Pritchard, Tim. *Ambush Alley: The Most Extraordinary Battle Of The Iraq War*. Presidio Press, 2005

Filkins, Dexter. *The Forever War*. Vintage Books, 2008

Remarque, Erich Maria. *All Quiet On The Western Front*. Ballantine Books–New York, 1982

Blehm, Eric. *The Only Thing Worth Dying For*. HarperCollins, 2010

Junger, Sebastian. *War*. Hatchette Book Group, 2010

North, Oliver. *American Heroes In Special Operations*. Fidelis Books, 2010

Darack, Ed. *Victory Point*. Berkley Caliber Books, 2009

Franzak, Michael. *A Nightmare's Prayer*. Threshold Editions/ Simon & Schuster, 2010

Davenport, Christian. *As You Were: To War and Back With the Black Hawk Battalion of the Virginia National Guard*. John Wiley & Sons, 2009

Weisskopf, Michael. *Blood Brothers*. Henry Holt and Company, 2006

Sasser, Charles W. *None Left Behind, The 10th Mountain Division and The Triangle Of Death*. St. Martins Press, 2009

Shaffer, Lt. Col. Anthony. *Operation Dark Heart*. St. Martins, 2010

Chasnoff, Joel. *The 188th Crybaby Brigade*. Free Press, 2010

Cambanis, Thanassis. *A Privilege To Die, Inside Hezbollah's Legions and Their Endless War Against Israel*. Free Press, 2010

Alexander, Matthew. *Kill or Capture, How a Special Operations Task Force Took Down A Notorious Al Qaeda Terrorist*. St. Martin's, 2011

Rosenberg, Joel C. *Inside the Revolution: How the Followers of Jihad, Jefferson & Jesus Are Battling to Dominate the Middle East and Transform The World*. Tyndale House, 2009

West, Bing. *The Wrong War*. Random House, 2012

Isby, David. *Afghanistan, Graveyard of Empires, A New History of the Borderland*. Pegasus Books, 2010

Peters, Ralph. *Endless War*. Stackpole Books, 2011

Smith, Lee. *The Strong Horse, Power, Politics, and The Clash Of Arab Civilizations*. Anchor Books, 2010

Workman, Jeremiah, with John R. Bruning. *Shadow of the Sword, A Marine's Journey of War, Heroism, and Redemption.* Presidio Press, 2009

Afong, Milo S. *Hunters, U.S. Snipers In The War On Terror.* Penguin Group, (USA) Inc., 2010

Kennedy, Kelly. *They Fought For Each Other.* St. Martin's, 2010

Parnell, Sean, with John Bruning. *Outlaw Platoon.* William Morrow/HarperCollins, 2012

Bradley, Major Rusty, and Kevin Maurer. *Lions of Kandahar.* Bantam Books, 2011

Weiss, Mitch, and Kevin Maurer. *No Way Out.* Berkley Caliber Books, 2012

Marlantes, Karl. *What It Is Like To Go To War.* Atlantic Monthly Press, 2011

Blehm, Eric. *Fearless.* WaterBrook Press, 2012

Couch, Dick. *Sua Ponte, The Forging Of A Modern American Ranger.* Berkley Books, 2012

Owen, Mark, with Kevin Maurer. *No Easy Day The Autobiography Of A Navy SEAL.* Penguin Group (USA), 2012

Wasdin, Howard E., and Stephen Templin. *SEAL TEAM SIX, Memoirs Of An Elite Navy SEAL Sniper*. St. Martins, 2011

Self, Nate. *TWO WARS*. Tyndale House, 2008

Webb, Brandon. *The Red Circle, My Life In The Navy SEAL Sniper Corps And How I Trained America's Deadliest Marksmen*. St. Martin's, 2012

Pfarrer, Chuck. *SEAL TARGET GERONIMO*. St. Martin's, 2011

Donald, Mark L., with Scott Mactavish. *Battle Ready, Memoir of a SEAL Warrior Medic*. St. Martin's, 2013

ACKNOWLEDGEMENTS

The very ones about whom this book is written are the ones who have contributed the most to it. The young combatants, medics, and others who physically, emotionally, and spiritually bear the brunt of the fight, have laid their lives on the line not primarily for the country, but for all of us... their people. They are, in infantry language, the "tip of the spear," and we are humbled and honored by their friendship, and taught by their dedicated lives.

I never dreamed of "writing a book," and was embarrassed when it was suggested. The thoughts I'd been writing down were for my own understanding and growth in ministry to combatants. As I wrote, I tested what I was learning for accuracy and usefulness through feedback from war-experienced friends, extending from young grunts to ranking line officers and chaplains.

It was Chaplain Mike Hoyt who began to press the book idea. I have such high regard for Mike's godly character and military stature that I felt compelled to consider the idea. I looked for input from other trusted military friends and was urged to follow Mike's advice. He then became a strong partner in writing what I finally acquiesced to calling a "book."

All this is simply to explain that, although I have no military credentials of my own other than having served for a few years as a Navy surgical tech, others whose military stature you may rely upon have scrutinized and contributed to the contents of the book. Below are listed a few of the trusted friends who have helped guide me in the writing, and have made contributions. All are equally committed to the spiritual welfare of soul-damaged warriors; and all have been personally touched by the soul-searing effects of war.

Colonel Mike Hoyt, Chaplain U.S. Army (Ret.). I met Mike and Judy and their girls at Ft. Drum, NY, where he served as Senior Chaplain for the 10th Mountain Division. He revealed himself to be not only an extremely effective chaplain leader, but also a compassionate friend who has ministered to Linda and me in ways we'll never forget. He has served as Senior Chaplain for Army Forces in Europe; Senior and Command Chaplain for all U.S. Forces in Iraq and on the personal staff of the Multinational Force-Iraq Commanding Generals; Director, Chaplain Corps Operations, Army Chief of Chaplains staff.

Colonel Dave Hale, U.S. Army (Ret.). I met Dave when he was a young Airborne officer in Vicenza, Italy, where he and Carole were a key part of our Hospitality House ministry. Walking with him and his family through his Army career has been a privilege and a remarkable ride. At the time of Dave's retirement, he was serving as Deputy Director, U.S. Army Intelligence and Security Command. His long and distinguished military career spans a wide variety of responsibilities, most of which could not be identified here, but has traversed many other special operations and intelligence commands.

Major Brian Koyn, Chaplain, U.S. Army. I met Brian when he was a reserve Army officer shepherding a fellowship of believers near Ft. Drum, NY. He sorted me out, labeled me as a "mentor," and we began to meet regularly, growing together in our respective ministries. Drawn back to active duty by the events of September 11, 2001, he furthered his theological training and became an Army chaplain. He served multiple deployments in Iraq and Afghanistan with the soldiers of the 82nd Airborne, and 1st Ranger Bn, and is presently the 75th Ranger Regimental Chaplain.

Major Matt Snell. I met Matt when, as a new Army infantry officer, he wheeled his pickup into the driveway of our Hospitality House at Ft. Drum, NY, and introduced himself as a follower of Christ. Matt and his wife, Meredith, quickly became close friends and a key part of our ministry. We were privileged to walk alongside them through the growth of their family and Army career. Being an infantry officer, Matt has served as an instructor at the Army Infantry Officer Basic Course; an infantry Company Commander in Balad, Iraq; a Brigade Battle Captain in Ramadi, Iraq; Chief of Operations of an Infantry Brigade in Paktika, Afghanistan; and as a Battalion Executive Officer in Afghanistan and in Germany.

Major Jason Farmer, U.S. Army, Foreign Area Officer. We "met" Jason through Matt Snell before he arrived at Ft. Drum as a new, single, infantry officer. We became friends right away and he, too, became a vital part of our Hospitality House ministry. We walked together as his career developed, and I well recall the conversation in which he told me of his intended move to Special Forces. More recently we've had the privilege of meeting his wife Bethany, and baby Lucie. After multiple combat tours and special educational preparation, Jason has achieved his desire — having grown up overseas in a missionary family — to become a Foreign Area Officer.

I've saved for last my acknowledgement of the most perfect partner in writing the book—my wife. In the last part of Genesis chapter 2, God describes how He formed woman as a "helper *suitable*" for her husband. He might as well have named her "Linda," and called it a day. As of this moment she has not even read this book, and yet she hasn't needed to. She has written it with me, by her life. She loved me and stood cheerfully beside me in the shattered streets of Vietnam and in the hard, rotten streets of Olongapo City, Philippines. She has helped me battle the cockroaches that snacked on our little boys as we made a house fit to serve the airmen and soldiers in Sattahib, Thailand. She has loved, welcomed, and served Army basic trainee retreat groups from Ft. Leonard Wood, and Army and Marine Corps Infantrymen at Ft. Drum and Camp Pendleton. She supported me while I traveled Asia and the Pacific for thirteen years, overseeing our Cadence workers there. There's no end to this, so I'll just stop with two more truths about my "suitable helper:" 1. In all this she has *never* complained against me or against God; *never* expressed a desire to quit or "go home;" never done anything but labor and love. 2. During all the time I've been learning to love combatants, she's been doing it instinctively.

CPSIA information can be obtained at www.ICGtesting.com
Printed in the USA
LVOW05s0616201113

361977LV00002B/128/P